Inside the Honey Walls

Dear Steve,

I think you will enjoy the book.

Sincerely

[signature]

Inside the Honey Walls

Using the mind tool of Meditation

C. J. Hoffman

iUniverse, Inc.
New York Bloomington Shanghai

Inside the Honey Walls
Using the mind tool of Meditation

iUniverse books may be ordered through booksellers or by contacting:

iUniverse
1663 Liberty Drive
Bloomington, IN 47403
www.iuniverse.com
1-800-Authors (1-800-288-4677)

Because of the dynamic nature of the Internet, any Web addresses or links contained in this book may have changed since publication and may no longer be valid.

The views expressed in this work are solely those of the author and do not necessarily reflect the views of the publisher, and the publisher hereby disclaims any responsibility for them.

ISBN: 978-0-595-48311-2 (pbk)
ISBN: 978-0-595-48902-2 (cloth)
ISBN: 978-0-595-60399-2 (ebk)

Printed in the United States of America

Thanks are extended to my family and friends for their assistance in proving to me, once again, that miracles and dreams do come true.

I love you all.

Contents

Introduction

Inside the Honey Walls is a very personal study. This book portrays the many and varied threads that were woven together in the course of my ongoing, personal search for ways to find joy and continuity in my life. These colorful threads gradually became a tapestry. And that tapestry enabled me to cope with a life that seemed broken from the beginning. It no longer mattered to me what outside influences swirled around me—and there were many I was determined to find a joyful and loving way to live, a way that nourished me. I found that meditation was an excellent way to accomplish that goal, and so I have practiced this master tool of restoration for most of my life.

To begin writing this memoir, I must return to my very early childhood. By the time I was seven years of age, I was struggling to give rise to a kind of understanding between any other person on this planet and myself. It was quite apparent that neither one of my parents would be that person. I rebelled when they misunderstood me and was punished for it, over and over.

In due course, I found that Grandma Hoffman, my Dad's mother, would be that person for that time in my life.

Everyone called her Katie, but her real name was Katrina. I thought she was the most beautiful grandmother I had ever seen. Her cloud of pure white hair was nestled closely to her head in a sort of halo, and her facial features were strong and sweet at the same time.

How I loved her, as she took me aside and pointed out the beauty that was in my world. She bought radiantly colored flowers and helped me to plant them in my yard. We sat together on long summer afternoons while we tried to make sense of the shapes in the fluffy white clouds moving in an azure sky. Seated on the front porch swing, we took in the smell of the clean air that surrounded us after a gentle rain, and we discovered that if we got up at daybreak and sneaked down beneath the giant trees in her yard, we could listen to the first robin wake up all the others and experience the cacophony of bird calls that it instigated.

She introduced such beauty into my young life, but most of all, I loved her for spending time with me.

Grandma and I played games. I sometimes play my favorite one with my own grandchildren. The game goes like this: Grandma would begin to tell an original story. After she had spoken for a few moments, she would suddenly point to me and I was to pick up the storyline, telling about three minutes of it before suddenly pointing back to her so she could continue the tale. We would do this pointing back and forth until the story became so ridiculous that we rolled with laughter, bringing the saga (for some of them were very long), to its required, hilarious ending.

When Grandma was not available to spend time with me, Grandpa Hoffman made it a point to do so. And, since they lived on the other side of our large double house on Briggs Street, this was an easy thing to do. I remember many times when he would find me alone swinging on the front porch swing. He would come to the banister and motion to me to come over to him, and he would lift me over the divider to his side of the porch.

Grandpa always had his two cocker spaniels, Timmy and Taffy, by his side. They were the drawing card for me to spend time with him. In fact, I remember him teasingly calling me Timmy, because my strawberry blond hair was the same color as Timmy's fur.

Grandpa and Grandma, in their own way, taught me that if I focused on the beauty and love that they supplied to my young life, it would give me joy to remind myself of it in the sad times. These remembrances were probably the beginnings of meditation for me, as I gradually learned to replace negative thoughts with positive ones.

The first chapter of my account, titled "Pretty Is as Pretty Does," tells a story that I remember from my early life about how I tried to resolve a problem I was having. You may not have had the same experience as I had. But please know that if you have had an experience of abuse, neglect, or failure to be understood in your childhood and it still bothers you as an adult, you may substitute your story for mine. The same meditation may be used as a template for your own story. You may take the journey back in time to the age of your abuse, for example, and from your adult vantage point, you will be able to purposefully soothe and love the little girl or boy that is in you. Meditating in this manner can finally establish in you the peace that you have longed for. You may be able, in time, to move from that hurtful place to live the awesome life that you were meant to live. The practice of meditation may do that for you.

Meditation takes practice and diligence. Ideally, the study of it involves more than perfunctory use. Meditation is a tool that requires handling and needs to be observed from all angles. Use it in as many life situations as possible, until it is as natural a function as eating and drinking. The practice of this tool truly does nourish you and builds your confidence in the actions you take, the words that you say, and the thoughts that you express to yourself.

The wisdom of meditation found me. I did not go looking for it. My grandparents taught me to replace negative thoughts with positive ones. The understanding that I gained from them sustained me through illness, abuse, and an attitude of angst that I did not belong on this earth plane. This last bit seemed to come to the surface when those people in my life that should have loved me the most, did not. I felt that I had so much love to give, and no one was there to accept it. This is one aspect of my life that cropped up time after time, forcing me to believe in karma (what goes around, comes around).

My fifth grade teacher, Miss Harris, and my grade school principal, Miss Johns, were my next mentors. They, perhaps inadvertently, taught me that my daydreams could have a correlation to real life. They set up the schedule for my school days to include painting a mural on the wall of a hall in our school building. It fulfilled many of my wishes including the daydream of having brothers and sisters who cared about me and would spend time with me doing those things we all enjoyed doing. Those childish meditations came to full fruit in the painting of the mural we later titled, "The History of Civilization". My dream of a family of brothers and sisters became the interaction with the other students in my class. We all had great fun together daubing colors on that giant mural. I remember that episode of my life as one of my happiest.

When I reached junior high school age, I began teaching other children in Sunday school at the Church of God, in the tiny town of Penbrook, Pennsylvania. I went through a loosely-put-together instruction for doing so, and I learned more about meditation. This meditation was not deep, but it was performed with love and evoked emotion and change nonetheless. It was called prayer. I was taught how to pray and when to pray. The practice of it added another level of benefit to me and to those for whom I prayed.

Some Christians in my church were sure that meditation was a pagan ritual. It was their position that if I had to bring up the subject, it should not be in Sunday school or church, and that was that! I did not argue with them for two reasons: they were my elders, and I knew for sure that the Bible that they used every Sunday was stuffed with references relating to meditation. I thought that they were in error at the time, and I still think that they missed out on a valuable resource for joy and strength.

After I married at the age of twenty, I read texts concerning comparative religions. I had access to these books because I had married a seminarian. He was a brilliant student, and I read what books on the subject of meditation I could glean from his large library. This added a mind full of information on the subject and considerably deepened my interest in it.

Since I was very busy with my babies and my duties at the church for the next five years, I practiced prayer, only taking the time to meditate when I was sure that I would be alone in the manse. I did not give up the practice, however, and when a high school student who occasionally visited our home brought me a gift of the Tao Te Ching (Dau De Jing), I was overjoyed.

The Tao was written by an ancient Chinese philosopher named Lao Tzu, who was keeper of the Imperial Library. Lao Tzu was famous for his wisdom concerning the best way to live one's life. That small book held a wealth of opportunity to search my soul and compare the thoughts I held to be true with those of the Tao. For instance, I held this to be true and still struggle with the concept: my religion holds that we must be strong in our faith, not bending like a reed with every wind that blows. The Tao says that those who bend in the wind will live to see another day, but those who are strong and do not bend will break and be useless.

A healing lesson of the Tao prescribes mental stimulation through meditation along with the well-known physical exercise known as the Chi Quong. Both of these disciplines are sensitive and deceptively simple, and they helped prepare me to live life to the fullest. There is so much to learn from the Tao that, in my opinion, it should be included in the library of every thinking person.

Over the last ten years, I have attended numerous philosophical discussions and seminars. Some of these have been as far away as Las Vegas and included thousands of students, while some have been as close to my home town of Palmyra, Pennsylvania, as the abutting city of Hershey and involved hundreds of students in seminars. Hummelstown, just a few miles down the road, has an even more intimate venue, where I study with perhaps a dozen other people once a month. Meditation has been a hot topic in all of these meetings, large and small.

I run the risk of going beyond my comfort zone at some of these seminars, especially at those that teach principles such as the value of past-life regression and how to use my animal guide to assist me in living a balanced and loving life. The latter was taught by an Indian shaman who somehow evoked from me a spider (my most feared nemesis), as my animal guide. After the selection of our animal guides, when we were asked to rise and share our experiences, I declined. It gave me a sense of having wasted my energy at the time, but soon I realized that these seminars gave me stark insight into the way my brain functions during meditation.

About seven years ago, in 2001, I was reintroduced to meditation for the performance of automatic writing. Automatic writing is also a mind tool, as is meditation, to access the subconscious part of our brain. It is a very simple way to discern your inner-most thoughts by putting pen to paper and writing down those things that come to mind. It is the focus of my first book, *The Joy Reminder*.

In May of 2002, confirmations were reintroduced to me. A confirmation is a thought, true or false, that is repeated time after time in your mind until you believe it to be true. It may be a negative one such as, "I am ugly", or a positive one such as, "I am beautiful." In any case it becomes what you believe and is translated from your subconscious to the way you live your life. Negative thoughts may color your life to the point of ruining it, if not replaced or overlaid with positive ones. I had practiced confirmations in my meditations in the late 1970s while going through a horrendous divorce. They were quite effective then, and consequently, now that I have been reminded of them, I am in the research stage of another book titled *An Elegant Echo* with that subject in mind. It will be written especially for you who need the comfort and the change of mind that confirmations bring in times of trouble.

In 2005, very specialized tutoring in the art of therapeutic touch and a course in Level One Reiki massage rounded out my knowledge of healing meditation techniques. This tutoring reminded me that the caring touch is beneficial to both the person being touched and to the person who touches them.

Inside the Honey Walls has been written carefully in a way that I feel will be most helpful to you. This book is composed of twelve chapters, and each chapter is divided into three parts. This was done in order to clarify the subject of meditation. I have written a story or parable in the beginning of each chapter. Contained in these stories are one or several ideas for your own future meditations. The second part of each chapter contains methods of preparation for that particular form of meditation. It also contains step-by-step instructions for the meditation. The third part of the chapter is the afterthought, which ties the story and the meditation together and gives you insight on ways to learn more about meditation from the chapter.

After you have read each chapter, you may want to return to the story and change it to fit an experience of your own. Please make the lessons in this book as personal as you require them to be, or learn from my experiences if they are close enough to your own experiences to make them valid for you.

In the end, I wanted these writings to be hard enough to make a point, but flexible enough to allow you to learn the practice of meditation on your own terms.

I do realize that some people who buy this book will read the stories and want nothing else from it. That is just fine by me, for this book is written for each one of you, and the value you place on each part of it is entirely up to you. All that I wish for you to see in this book are the joy and love with which it was written to you.

—C. J. Hoffman

Preface

Meditation is the ability to focus to the extent that you transcend rational, everyday thought. Clearing your mind in this way enables you to access the subconscious, where truth and wisdom are stored. It allows you relax, find comfort, and solve problems.

One way to practice the skill of the focused thought is to be cognizant of your breathing. This is a pure and natural way to begin:

- Close your eyes as you breathe slowly in and out, your mind tuned only to your breath.

- Set your intention on the attainment of a clear mind. If your mind strays to something other than the in and out of your breathing, you will simply acknowledge the thought and return to the breathing exercise. This is probably the most difficult hurdle to jump, but with practice, you can do it.

- When you have cleared your mind of the ideas and situations that flit through it constantly and your thoughts are firmly fixed on the in and out of your breathing, you will begin the meditation. If you wish, you may practice this breathing technique, which is the point of focus in meditation, in advance of reading the stories and meditations in this book.

Each meditation will coincide with the story or parable preceding it and will be unique. I will guide you—or more accurately, write for you—the instructions to move you along in the meditation.

You may dig deeply into your soul to resolve what you think are latent issues, only to find that they are not as dormant as you thought. Perhaps you will forgive in an instance when you neglected to do so in the past, or you may touch on what your talents are. I am sure that you are anxious to query for yourself some of your life's mysteries. Trust that you will be awed by the results of your meditative work.

As you delve into the stories and corresponding meditations contained in this book, I instruct you in deeper ways to achieve meditation. A slightly different approach is used for each chapter.

I will lead you through every practice meditation, step by step. The first meditations are simple and short in duration, but they contain many instructions for your success. These meditations concern the events of childhood, and they are written to be generally useful.

As I age in the progression of stories, the meditations reflect that. They become somewhat longer in length and denser in complexity. There are four types of meditation positions that I have personally explored, and I will address each of them with some explanation as to my experience with them:

- The *walking* meditation, in practice, is using conscious meditation while walking slowly back and forth in a straight line. The act of meditation is awareness of your subconscious and how it relates to your body and mind. No matter the method or pose for the meditation, this is a constant. You may use a variation of this form of meditation by walking in a large circle, while maintaining the same mindset as previously described. I frequently practice walking the quiet streets of my neighborhood with my focus on my actions and how they relate to my environment. When you do this, you must be certain that the environment is a safe one, for you will not be aware of anything outside your meditation. You may not hear a car coming, for instance, because your conscious senses are suspended while you are in meditation. You may liken this state of being to reading a very good book that you are totally immersed in. A person near to you in the same room may speak to you, but you are unaware of it. You cannot hear it. The walking meditation is a happy alternative for those who find that sitting for periods of time is uncomfortable and for those of us that are more hyper and energetic than others.

- The *standing* meditation is just what it sounds like—meditation while standing. It can lead to deep awareness as you notice how your feet interact with the ground and know that you are standing in balance. You are aware of the way the separate parts of your body work together to keep you upright and balanced. The standing meditation can easily be combined with walking meditations, and we will do that as one of our exercises.

- The *sitting* meditation allows for you to sit in a chair with hands on your thighs and feet solidly placed on the floor. It also permits you to sit on the floor or the ground with your legs tucked in the lotus position, which folds one leg tightly over the other. Most westerners sit with legs simply folded in front of them. The sitting meditation is my favorite, but I vary the pose from time to time. I usually use the sitting pose when I feel that the meditation will be an extended one and that I will grow weary practicing the walking or the standing meditation. The sitting position will preclude interruption of the meditation for this reason.

- The *lying* meditation is one that I learned from information on the Internet when I had a large synovial cyst in my spine. The pain had become great, and I could no longer function in the standing, sitting, or walking poses for my meditation. The lying pose was a great help to me and allowed me to fall asleep more easily, as it seemed to ease my pain. It is also useful for someone who is ill, aged, or too obese to comfortably perform the other positions. When I am having problems sleeping, this position is very beneficial. Lie gently on your right side, place your right palm under your face, and position your left arm and hand along the left side of your body. Drape your left leg loosely over your right one and you are in place, ready to begin the focus exercises.

Meditation is an ancient form of accessing wisdom and truth. It is also a very modern tool for reaching within yourself to your subconscious, that part of your psyche that keeps track of your total life experience and where we all begin knowledge of this life.

People of all major religions meditate, sometimes in the form of prayers. Atheists meditate also, hinting that meditation has not much to do with religion. But I am sure in my heart that meditation, the tool that enables us to touch knowledge and absorb wisdom from the Source of our being, is a masterful discipline to practice. I pray that *Inside the Honey Walls* will touch your heart and that you will begin the practice of meditation.

Chapter 1

Pretty Is as Pretty Does

"Stinking buses," I thought. "Those stinking, rotten buses"! I said under my breath as I stubbed the toe of my good patent leather shoe on the cement sidewalk.

The bare truth was that I was in a stinking, rotten snit and Mother was very angry at me. She held my left hand so tightly that it went numb, and once in a while, she looked in my direction with that blue-eyed, warning stare of hers. Occasionally, she tried to smile at passersby. Normalcy was what she was trying for, I guess, and I was having none of it as I struggled to free my hand from her grip.

We were waiting at the corner of Main and 19th Street for the city bus, my nemesis. I would have walked the mile to Harrisburg, but Mother was adamant about taking the bus.

When the green and silver monster finally roared to the curb and the driver whooshed open the bi-fold doors, I knew I was defeated. I was seven years old, and Mother knew that I could control my bodily functions in a more ladylike fashion than the last dozen times or more that I journeyed on the bus. Could she not remember previous bus rides when she had to stand up in mid-block in order to pull the emergency cord for me to debark and throw up in the gutter? That act was very disturbing to me on so many levels that it was difficult for me to forget.

Mother pushed me gently ahead of her as we climbed the rubber-coated steps to the driver's seat where there was a shiny metal box. She deposited the fare for the two of us in it, and a tiny bell rang as each nickel was registered as payment.

I quickly surveyed the bus and my heart sank. I was hoping for a seat near the front so that I could gulp fresh air every time those blessed doors opened for another fare, but the bus was crowded.

With my last hope gone, Mother put her fingers in the middle of my back and steered me to the back of the bus, where one and a half seats were waiting for us on the bench. I wedged myself into the space allotted me. There happened to be a drunk on my right, a nice, older woman on his right, and Mother was on my left side.

Mother sat conveniently under the emergency cord, but she was staring straight ahead with her jaw set. I knew that look well. It was her "don't you dare say a word to me," look. The wire was much too high for me to reach, and Mother did not seem amenable to pulling it, even if my situation required such a move on her part.

In desperation, I moved on to plan B. I would try to control the urge I felt to get out of this situation by concentrating very hard on watching the houses, yards, and the happy children who played in them. I would try to remember what Grandma Hoffman taught me. She assured me that when I was in a tough position, I could look outside of the situation to something beautiful or I could think of a time when I was really happy. This would make me forget the bad things and remember only the good ones.

We passed many white cottages with blue or green shutters at the windows. The yards surrounding them teemed with happy, playing children. I really tried to focus on all the laughter and fun that they were having, but the thoughts that crowded my mind were how none of those children were sitting between an angry mother and a now-leaning drunk and being stared at by a little old lady, all while trapped in the back of a hot, stinking bus. Oh no—they were allowed to play outdoors in the sunshine and fresh air. Well, so much for plan B, since that idea made me yearn to escape right then and there, adding to my predicament.

Plan C was to somehow control the bile I felt rising in my throat. I was in real pain, but I concentrated on keeping it in check.

A few blocks had passed when the older lady sitting next to the now-sleeping drunk leaned forward in her seat far enough to get the attention of my mother.

"What a pretty daughter you have," she said with a sweet smile.

Mother hesitated just long enough for me to take in the compliment and then answered, "Pretty is as pretty does," as she returned to her forward stare.

Well that was that. I leaned back on the slippery green plastic seat and swallowed hard. I had embarrassed her, and now Mother was so angry with me that she would not look my way no matter how long I gazed longingly at her.

Feeling sorry for myself and for my actions at the bus stop, I went back to concentration mode as I began feeling dizzy. I recognized dizziness as the feeling that was the precursor to everything else that could happen.

Our bus stop finally loomed in the near distance, and Mother stood to pull the cord that was my ticket out of there and to fresh air. The bus came to a stuttering halt. I dashed to the back doors, pushed in front of everyone else, and ran down the rubber-coated steps, jumping the last one to land on the sidewalk. When Mother finally debarked after letting everyone else off the bus ahead of her, she looked at me in utter disgust. If looks could have killed, I would have been lying there on the concrete.

Mother angrily grabbed my hand and off we strode to Pomeroy's Department Store as I consoled myself with the thought that plan C really did work.

Certainly all was not forgiven. I would be punished when I got home and Mother told Dad about all that happened on our shopping trip.

I would certainly have to prepare myself for the next bus trip that we would have together, and I considered talking the matter over with Grandma before that time came. Thankfully, though, Dad was picking us up on Market Square at four o'clock, so that bus ride would not be today.

The Sitting Meditation

Preparation:

- Pray for clarity as you receive positive confirmation that you are able to change your life through meditation.

- Prepare a clean, quiet room with a mat or clean rug for you to sit on.

- Choose background music that is calm and soothing.

- Draw curtains or blinds, if possible, and close the door to foot traffic. Place a simply written note on the door with the words, "meditating, please do not disturb" on it.

- Light a small candle and place it in front of your mat.

- Try sitting down on your mat in lotus position, or cross your legs in front of you. If this is uncomfortable, sit on a folded blanket or a flat cushion.

- Check your clothing for softness and make sure your clothes are comfortable, especially around the waist.

- Relax your head on your chest and slowly raise it three times, or until the tension eases in your neck muscles, while continuing to exhale and inhale.

- Take seven slow, deep breaths.

- On the eighth breath, watch your tummy expand as you inhale and watch your tummy deflate as you exhale.

- If you find that your tummy deflates when you inhale and expands when you exhale, you are breathing incorrectly.

- Practice the correct way of breathing, tummy expanding on the inhale and deflating on the exhale, for a few moments until you find success in this process. It is important that you learn the natural way to breathe, for it is the way you breathed as a baby.

- Pay close attention to your breath as you slowly and deeply breathe in and out. Your mind is calm and your breath is your focus.

Begin the meditation

- You are in the meditative state.

- The subject for meditation is your own uncomfortable situation that you experienced as a child.

- You will now undertake your journey back in time. You have done this before—in thought, if not in meditation.

- As you slowly move along your backward path through time, experience by experience confronts you and then passes in front of you as you feel the emotions of each encounter.

- One scene is you at eighteen years of age. You are very secure in your skin. See yourself smiling and sure-footed in your social life. You fear very little at this age. Observe yourself as you pass by on your way to the next point of reference.

- You fade backward four years and arrive at the front of your home room. You are in the ninth grade.

- Are you more secure or less secure as you become younger?

- Picture yourself at the age of fourteen, standing at the blackboard working an algebra problem.

- Feel those teenage feelings caused by normal body changes. Do these transformations cause you to be awkward and shy? I know that you would like to spend more time with yourself at this age. You seem so vulnerable, and looking back now, you could use your adult experience as comfort.

- Remember that you may pause anywhere in time that you wish, only keep your childhood destination in mind.

- Continue backward in time until you reach seven years of age. Feel the feelings of yourself as a child. You may be forty or so inches tall or a bit gangly, but you know how you look, you know how you feel, and according to your particular story, you have a problem that stems from a situation you found yourself in as a young child. Enjoy this little girl or boy. Take the time to play before you push on. You know the reason you came to this childhood place. You have a problem to solve. In your story, something very painful occurred and you do not want to repeat that pain.

- When you are ready, envision your perception of the attack on your youthful sensibilities. The situation reveals itself exactly as you remembered it.

- This time, you walk over to the source of your downfall. Confront it as you would have if you had been an adult and not a child at the time of your attack.

- Speak to the attacker in adult language. There may be some strong language that you need to use to solve the situation.

- You will act in a way that shows you are now fearless, and that the attack will never happen again.

- You are confident that you no longer fear the situation.

- Walk around the field of attack, whatever it may be, and see that the fearful situation has been put to ruin by your words and actions.

- There is no longer a threat before you, only a poor example of the human condition.

- You are no longer afraid of the scene before you and you may experience pity for it.

- Train your vision on the pitiful situation before you. Remember it well, for it will never again be the fearful problem it once was.

- When you are ready, you will travel forward in time, just as you traveled backward in time, slowly.

- Each meeting of yourself as a younger person will again pass before your eyes. You will feel renewed happiness or sorrow with each meeting. Do not be afraid of your emotion; it is a vital part of your healing.

- As you find yourself nearing the present, you will feel comfortable and loved. Smile as you open your eyes to a new and fearless life.

Afterthought

In the preceding story, I was on the right track with plan B—distracting myself by watching happy scenes outside the bus—but I lost my focus. I resorted to something I knew would work most of the time, pure willpower. Even though I knew it would be more difficult to take the willpower route, I panicked. Instead of retrieving my focus and continuing the plan B meditation, I chose the lesser of the disciplines for my use.

If you are bothered by a fear that began in childhood, as most of us are, you may use this meditation as an example for a way to expel your own fears. What has always been amazing to me is the way that adult fears can be eradicated by the death of the childish fear. I have suffered from motion sickness since childhood, and I return to my own meditation from time to time for a refresher course. Please return to this meditation any time you wish, because fear is sometimes difficult to eradicate.

Chapter 2

Park Your Carcass Park

Dad was not an astute businessman, but he was addicted to business partnerships. He always had some venture going, and since he loved the out-of-doors, it usually was something to do with hunting or fishing. The most interesting scheme, though, had to do with Mr. Gorham.

Dad was thirty-eight at the time—and I was eight years old—when Mr. Gorham, a self-styled businessman, came into our lives. He passed himself off as a Southern colonel, which even I knew to be untrue. He had not an ounce of politeness in him, was rather gruff, and lacked a Southern drawl. Nope, he was not the real deal as far as I was concerned.

I do not know who sucked whom into this crazy idea, but they both seemed excited about it, and this is how Park Your Carcass Park came into the planning stage.

Mr. Gorham had bought a tract of farmland north of Harrisburg, near the small town of Halifax. It had a house and a barn on it. His plan was for our whole family to move there from our home in the city. We were to farm a vegetable patch and raise chickens, geese, pigs, and ducks for food. The first two parts of the plan dealt with something completely foreign to all of us. But, Dad unilaterally decided it was a great idea.

Dad had made plans that included his friend Leo, and as soon as I was out of school in the spring, he and Leo who was not a part of the scheme, only an innocent bystander, were going to pack us up and move the whole family to Mr. Gorham's farm.

It was one of the stupidest ideas I had ever heard of, so I had my own plan all settled in my mind. The plan was that I would live with Grandma and Grandpa Hoffman. They conveniently resided next door to us, in Harrisburg. My family could move if they wanted to, but I was not budging.

When I told him how I wanted things to happen, Dad thought that was a crazy idea. On moving day, when I was forced into the cab of the black Ford pickup loaded with boxes and topped with some of our furniture, I had a raging fit about leaving and ended up being punished. It appeared that moving to that God-forsaken place out of town was not punishment enough.

The road trip to Halifax took forever, although in fact it was probably less than an hour's journey. When we drove up in front of our new home and Dad killed the engine on the truck, we all just sat there and looked to our left in horror. Leo drove up in back of us and, not bothering to kill the motor on his truck, drew up beside us with a sorry look on his face.

I did not believe that any of us could imagine that we were going to live there, including Dad. The house was definitely leaning to the right, and it was way beyond being a fixer-upper. There were a few outbuildings in back of the barn that actually looked more stable than the house, but the barn was not one of them. Looking around me, I began comparing every structure to that run-down house.

When I announced that I had to use the bathroom, I was ushered down the path beside the house to what I thought must be a play house. It wasn't.

We moved in that day. Dad's friend Leo could not stop shaking his head as he off-loaded our boxes from his overloaded truck. When he finished the chore, he got into his dilapidated vehicle, revved the engine, and roared out of there without saying good-bye. Dad watched this all play out and stared down that dusty dirt road long after his friend was out of sight. "This is not good," I thought as I continued carrying boxes from the front porch into the house.

I swear that the day we moved in that house, which we tried to make a home, was the day that Mother began having debilitating headaches. For days at a time she would hardly be able to hold her head erect, and the headaches did not subside until she moved out of Halifax, two and a half years later. I had tried to console her, but the pain on the top of her head made her grouchy, and she would shoo me away.

I spent a lot of my time after doing my chores seated on the porch steps, watching my brother and sister do tumbles down the grassy, sloping yard beside the house. At the ripe old ages of three and four, they seemed to be the only ones having fun.

One day, I decided that I could use some of that joy, which seemed to refresh itself every morning from a bottomless pit deep inside them. So the next day, after the eggs were collected and I had completed my chores, I sauntered out the front door of the house around to the west side of it and walked beneath the giant pine trees that grew there. My sister and brother were playing on the opposite side of the house and I could barely hear them, so this was prime time for me to get started. I was determined to find the happy place that my siblings enjoyed, and I named the pursuit of it my Joy project.

I surveyed the area, hoping to find one of those astonishingly beautiful, shiny, blue-black lizards that sometimes slithered among the cool needles shed from the pines. But, I was alone.

Scooping up some of the soft, slim leaves, I built a pile of them. I planned to sit beside the small rill that ran the depth of the property and emptied into a wide creek that was the southern boundary of the farm.

I sat down on the fragrant, pine-smelling mound with my legs crossed and my back straight. It was the way I liked to sit, and the position was fairly comfortable for me.

The rill made faint burbling sounds, and I listened intently as the robins sang their "Cherrie, Cherrie" bird song. I was very content. The sounds of the rill and the robins may have been enough to fulfill the joy quotient for that day, but what about the next one, and the next? As much as the sounds and smells appealed to me, I concluded that this was not the solution to the Joy project.

Every day, I wanted to get awake and be happy. I did not want to hunt for the joy, as I had done that day. I wanted it to just be there, waiting for me to awaken in the morning.

My thoughts were interrupted when I heard Mother calling from the back porch that dinner was ready. "Come in to wash up," she called, as an afterthought.

I met my brother and sister as they came running toward the front of the house and held the rickety screen door as they bolted through it, heading for the basin of water in the drysink. My Joy project would have to wait, for immediately after dinner, I had more chores to do.

Dad came in to wash his hands in the sudsy basin of water while we were clearing the table. Mother reheated the meat and potatoes for him, and he sat down to eat. He was late because he had taken the time to free Major, our mahogany-hued stallion, from the cultivator. He had washed him down and given him a few carrots and some water. Dad loved horses, which was the only reason he had joined the cavalry in World War II. He loved Major in particular.

There was just one problem with that relationship. Nearly every day since Major was installed as the only horse on the farm, he kicked his way out of the stable and hightailed it to the nearest neighbor's field. He would proceed to do as much damage as he could to the crop that was planted there before Dad, huffing and puffing, could catch up with him.

If the field Major had chosen was a wheat field, he could be seen in the distance, turning round and round, his giant hooves stamping the grain in ever-widening circles. If a cornfield was Major's choice for the day, he would unceremoniously take the cornstalks in his enormous teeth and break them off about halfway to the ground. He sometimes took out most of a row before Dad noticed that he was gone and ran in his direction. And so it went, day after day, they would play this game that Dad always lost.

In Dad's defense, he tried everything he could think of to restrain Major. He roped him to a ring at the back of the stall. He screwed boards, left over from one of his projects, across the door, which gave him another level of work to do: he'd have to unscrew the boards in order to take care of the horse. Nothing worked. Major was so big and so strong-willed that I know he could have made a horse-shaped hole in the side of the barn, just to run free.

One day, Major was acting in a particularly odious manner. He had broken out of his confinement and this time was found munching on the vegetables in a neighbor's truck patch. That garden happened to be right outside Mrs. Shoop's kitchen door.

To make matters even more interesting, Major had knocked down the surrounding fence to gain entrance to the garden. Dad was already doing the math for its replacement when the horse strayed out of Mrs. Shoop's view from the kitchen and Dad snagged him. He swung a leg over that horse's back and rode him back home as hard as he could.

I was on the front porch shucking corn when they pulled up on Major's hind legs. "I'm going to ride this horse until he drops," Dad shouted to no one in particular. And, holding to the leather strap he had fastened around Major's muscular neck, he rode hell-bent down the dirt road and disappeared in a cloud of dust.

No less than an hour later, Major came prancing back to the front porch as if he were a show horse. Dad, on the contrary, slid off that stallion's back as soon as he came to a stop. The horse knew he owned the victory. As for Dad, what he mumbled is far better left unwritten.

Major liked to drink from the sweet spring in Park Your Carcass Park, and after this ride he headed for it. The development of Park Your Carcass Park and that spring into a spa was the next proposed component in Mr. Gorham's plan, so we tried to keep the bubbling water source covered. Our stallion sauntered across the road to it, nudged the round of wood that covered the spring, and drank his fill, just because he could.

Dad did not have much to say to or about Major after that day, except gee and haw, when the horse was hitched to the cultivator. Dad did cuss at him in frustration, though as he tried to keep him lined up between the rows of vegetables. But Major always did his own thing, which was tramping down most of them.

You could tell that Major loved Dad, for he would try to nuzzle him for the treats that Dad usually kept in his deep pockets just for him. And then, finding no treats, he would ceremoniously prop his big head on Dad's shoulder and mournfully stare into the distance.

After the incident in Mrs. Shoop's garden, Major suddenly stopped kicking his way out of the stable. I chose to think that he knew that he had finally crossed the line with Dad and was trying to make up for it. But, the horse that could not stop horsing around was sold soon after that. Dad and Major both despaired the day of their parting, but part they did. No one seemed to understand exactly what happened there, but I saw that when a man and his beloved animal ceased to understand each other, it was the end of the relationship. It was sad to witness.

Speaking of understanding each other, we humans sometimes defy understanding. One day, Mr. Gorham made one of his bimonthly visits to the farm. He wore his white suit and carried his fancy cane on his sleeve. It was to be his last visit, for he had decided that he was no longer interested in developing the sweet spring on that property into the spa that he and Dad had oddly named Park Your Carcass Park. All of Dad's work clearing the land and redoing the outbuildings were all for nothing. After that, he headed for greener pastures, I would assume. Dad's partner sold the property and never looked back.

We were all disheartened by this turn of events, but Dad took our situation hard, since it was his determination that brought us to this place, and he started drinking again. Things went downhill after that. We had no place to live and not much money. The Joy project seemed like a useless dream to me then, as we did our best to survive.

The Lying Meditation

Preparation:

• Pray that only positive things will be shown to you in your meditation.

• Decide where you are going to perform the lying meditation. For example, you may lie on the grass outside, inside on a rug, or on your bed. If you choose the bed for your meditation, a firm mattress is best, to give maximum support to your body while you meditate.

- Wear soft, loose-fitting clothes.

- Lie down gently on your right side.

- Place your right palm under the right side of your face. Ask yourself if this is comfortable, and if you are not comfortable, gently adjust your body until you are.

- Position your left arm and hand along the left side of your body.

- Drape your left leg loosely over your right one with your knee bent.

- If this position feels calming to you, you are ready to begin the focus exercise.

Begin the meditation

- Close your eyes. Imagine a faraway point of light. Focus only on that light.

- If your mind is crowded with thoughts, acknowledge them, and return to that bright point of light. Practice this as many times as you require.

- When you are able to focus only on the light, begin pulling it closer to you until it fills you with its radiance. This may be difficult to understand until you actually do it. Your subconscious mind works for you just as you request it to do.

- The radiance of that light is your joy. Imagine it and name it Joy. You will remember this light or spark of light every time you have need of it.

- Imagine awakening to the light. Your light does not equate to sunlight, for it is always there for you.

- Resolve to request this light before you go to sleep each night, and it will be there for you in the morning. Train your conscious mind in this way to look for the light and acknowledge it.

- Remember from this time on to call that light Joy.

- If you have not fallen asleep during this short but important meditation, you will tell yourself to slowly open your eyes and be at peace.

- Do not be concerned if you fall asleep while meditating. The meditation will continue while you sleep, and if you acknowledge your joy in the morning, you will experience it just the same.

Afterthought

How odd it is that when you would benefit most from experiencing joy, you sometimes consider it a frivolous distraction. The story above certainly points that out for you because, in the end, I gave up the search for joy in order to simply survive.

A few years passed before I resumed my search for my own personal joy, and at that time I was successful in finding it. The spark has never dimmed from that time to this, and I feel eternally grateful for that gift.

There is material for at least one other meditation in the story written above. If you wish, you may develop a simple meditation of your own. Perhaps it will have as its subject understanding others, or understanding animals. I do hope that you benefit from this simple story in a most unusual way.

Chapter 3

Painting the History of Civilization

When I was ten, I left my farm home, my family, and a one-room schoolhouse back in Halifax to travel south to a suburb of Harrisburg. I had lived in the city of Harrisburg, Pennsylvania, from the time I was born until the age of eight, and I was happy to be back.

The reason for the sudden move was that my parents had "farmed me out" to an elderly couple, Mr. and Mrs. Taylor, who would extend food and shelter to me in exchange for housework and help with the cooking. All this was news to me when my bags were packed and I was summarily delivered to the Taylors' back door one Sunday evening in early September.

When I arrived at their tidy white cottage, Mr. and Mrs. Taylor did not speak, but they showed me and my bags to my tidy room immediately. I thanked Mrs. Taylor, and they quickly closed the door. Oddly enough, the thing I remember most about that first evening was that the two of them walked in tandem, as if somehow hitched to each other.

I upended my two brown paper bags on the worn white bedspread in order to choose an outfit to wear the next day. I was told it was to be my first day at Progress Elementary School.

The events of the day happened in quick succession, but I was eager for the change—in fact, I found it to be exciting.

Not long after I began unpacking, Mrs. Taylor rapped on the door and poked her white-haired head around the corner to where I was standing in front of the closet. I was hanging my meager wardrobe on the hangers she had provided, and I stepped out into the room to see what she wanted.

She had a snack of milk in one hand and a piece of chocolate cake on a fancy plate in the other. She handed them across the bed to me and, saying nothing, waited, watching me as I took my first forkful of cake. I followed it with a sip of milk and smiled at her in appreciation. If she was not talking, neither was I.

On the road trip to my new home, I had been admonished to remember my manners. I guessed that was what Mother meant—speak only when you are spoken to.

Evidently satisfied that I was enjoying the treat, Mrs. Taylor retreated and quietly closed the door, leaving me to finish eating the food she had provided, or not.

I saved a bit of the cake for later, but drank the whole glassful of the cool, creamy milk. Probably, no one thought to tell her that I was allergic to milk, and therefore craved it. I did not say a word about it either, since it seemed that no one was allowed to speak in this house. In the middle of the night, I was paid back for my oversight.

I had read of the bends that plagued divers when they came to the surface of the water too quickly, and I likened that to the terrible cramps that rippled my abdomen. They continued for hours, and I finally cried myself to sleep as daylight became visible through the curtains of the one small window in my bedroom.

A few hours later, I was awakened by a soft rap on the door and another peek around the corner. I sat up, still half asleep, and found myself staring into a small mirror on the wall at the foot of the bed. I hardly recognized myself. My eyes were slits in the balloon that was now my face.

Mrs. Taylor looked a bit concerned at this turn of events, but said not a word. I smiled weakly in her direction. She made sure that I was awake, which was her purpose in knocking on the door in the first place and quietly closed the door.

Hopping out over the side of the bed, I took the washcloth and towel that were draped over the foot of it and walked across the hall to the bathroom, where I cleaned up and scrubbed my teeth. I felt very unwell, to say the least, as I wandered back into the bedroom to get dressed for school.

It did not take long for me to put on the white blouse and gathered skirt that Mother had sewn for me out of cloth feed bags. The skirt was blue with tiny white dots sprinkled all over it, and I liked it a lot. I finished off this outfit with white socks and the only pair of shoes I owned. I felt chilly, and quickly threw on a blue sweater over the short-sleeved blouse. I opened the door and headed toward the smell of food coming from the cramped kitchen. "I will be happy here," I promised myself.

The Taylors, who had obviously already eaten, shuffled past me in the hall. I backed myself against the wall as they passed, still walking in tandem. They were headed to the sunroom at the front of the cottage, to read the papers they had tucked beneath their arms.

A few steps later, I entered the kitchen and helped myself to the three strips of bacon and one piece of toast that had been left on a plate for me. I noticed that there was a glass of water poured for me, instead of the milk I might have expected. It seemed that the Taylors were on to the allergy thing and that I could expect no more milk from them.

After I finished breakfast, I wriggled out of my seat at the table and took my dishes to the sink where a basin of hot, sudsy water was waiting.

I washed the dishes, rinsed, and dried them. I made a neat little stack of plates on the counter and lined up the glasses in a row in back of them. The knives and forks sat gleaming to one side. I would learn where they belonged later.

I emptied and rinsed the basin I had washed the dishes in and hung it on a small nail beside the kitchen door. I had noticed the basin hanging there when I arrived the night before.

A loud knock on the kitchen door startled me, and then I remembered that Dad had promised to come by and drive me to school early so that he could register me. I opened the door for him and he took one look at me, and then looked down at his shoes. All he could think to do was shake his head. I felt as if I had stepped into a warp zone where everyone had forgotten how to talk—first the Taylors, and now Dad.

I did not say a thing about what I might have done to deserve my appearance, but of course he knew. He put his hand in the middle of my back and shoved me toward the door and the whole way to his truck. I got into my side and adjusted my skirt so that it would not wrinkle as he stomped around the front of the Ford. He climbed in and we sped out the stony driveway in reverse.

After a short, fast drive up Colonial Road and out 39th Street, we turned right onto Route 22. There was not much traffic, so Dad did not hesitate to speed around the corner, putting us on 34th Street. In no time at all, we came to a bone-jarring stop in front of *Progress Elementary School.*

The school was three stories high, built of red brick, and trimmed in white. There were six tall windows in front, and a brown, wooden double door that allowed for the many children that I was sure attended there. If it were possible to love a building, I fell for that one.

I opened the door of the truck and jumped out. Dad climbed out his side and strode ahead of me, up a few steps, opened one side of the door, and entered.

The heavy, wooden door had almost closed by the time I got there, but I caught it before it slammed. I walked into the school, up the steps, and ran to catch up with Dad, who was already halfway to the office at the end of the hall.

We entered the outer office together and walked up to the desk. Dad reminded the secretary that he had called the previous Friday to tell her that we would be registering today, so they must be expecting us.

He filled out a few questions, signed his name on a sheet of paper, and was off, out of office, down the hall, and out the double doors. I was not there to catch it this time and I heard it close, hard. When I turned back to her desk, the young woman got up, took me by the arm, and we headed upstairs to my classroom.

It was almost deserted, since I had arrived an hour before the bell was to ring. That extra hour gave Dad time to get to work on time—he was a boxcar brakeman at the Enola train yards.

The teacher was already seated at her desk at the head of the room. She looked up from her book and motioned for me to sit in one of the front seats, which I obediently did.

"Well, welcome to Progress Elementary School," I said under my breath, feeling a snit coming on.

Partly because of my initial attitude (the snit refused to abate), attending my new school soon became problematic, and after only a week Miss Johns, my teacher, submitted a request to Principal Harris. She asked that I be evaluated for matriculation to the next grade.

When notified of the plan, Dad turned absolutely purple at the thought. He gave as his reason for vetoing the idea that I was already one year younger than most of the other students in my grade. It did not matter one bit to him that I had been taught most of my current lessons the year before, and therefore I languished in the fifth grade, bored out of my skull.

To alleviate that boredom, I drummed on the edge of my desk with my pencil, talked to the girl next to me until we both got in trouble, and read a book I borrowed from the boy seated in front of me. This last try at sanity seemed to be a very large indiscretion, for the book was taken away from the both of us until the end of the day, when the lender was told to take the book home and not to bring it back.

My teacher did try to help me, but with forty other children to teach, the only innocuous endeavor she could think of was to see that I had extra paper and was given crayons to draw with. When the other children complained about the special treatment, however, she removed them from my desk.

With all the other alternatives gone from my stable of things to keep me awake, I resorted to focusing my attention out those high, grand windows. I enjoyed creating tableaux populated with cloud people and animals. They passed by my field of vision, became part of the blue expanse of sky for a moment, and then moved on. I became indifferent to what was happening in the classroom and was in another world. And, in that world that I created, I was at peace.

I soon became adept at using my sky focus during these daydreams to create an altered life for myself. My new daydreams were populated by families consisting of my many brothers and sisters who played and sang songs with me. In turn, I read them stories and played the piano for them. In a very short time, I created a loving and joyful life for myself. Miss Johns, I am sure, concluded that a quiet, daydreaming child was better than a disruptive one, and left me to my own devices.

One day about three months into the school term, I was called to the principal's office. I froze when I heard my name over the loudspeaker. I had just come in from recess and was still red-faced and breathing hard from playing tag.

Seeing that I would not or could not move, Miss Johns walked to my desk and escorted me out the door and down two flights of stairs to the longest hall I ever walked. She rapped on the partially open office door to let Miss Harris know that we had arrived. She gently nudged me through the door and stood me in front of the principal's desk.

Miss Harris did not immediately raise her head from the papers she was reading, which gave me a bit of time to overcome my nerves. I felt that this time I may have done something or other and would be sent home to explain myself to the Taylors. That would be a pain in the neck because the two of them had not given up their silence. In fact, they rarely made any sound and had obviously decided that nods and headshakes were sufficient to converse with a ten-year-old.

I soon discovered that the subject of this meeting was not my deportment, as the principal and Miss Johns began to outline a special plan they had for me. This plan was obviously engineered for the sanity of everyone involved with my education. They noticed and sympathized with the fact that I was bored to distraction, and they figured out an alternative way to handle my situation.

The plan was to see that my school experience was as positive as possible. It was a plan so out of the box, for those times, that it amazes me still. Those great educators arranged for me to take advanced classes in history and art—my two favorite subjects—three mornings a week. Additionally, I would teach remedial reading to second graders the remaining two mornings. Best of all, after my lessons had been completed for the day, I would spend part of each afternoon researching and painting a mural of the history of civilization on the walls of the hall I had just nervously trod. Miss Harris and Miss Johns rightly figured that I had no outside access to books, so they saw to it that I had at my disposal the use of an assortment of world history books.

This plan was the greatest gift I ever received. I managed to say thank you to them both, but not much sound found its way around the lump in my throat.

You have to search, even today, for educators more committed to their students than Miss Johns and Miss Harris. I never forgot their kindness or their dedication to their students and their profession.

I researched and painted, taught and was taught. It was a joyful time in my life.

Other young people in my class joined me at the wall to paint the history of civilization. They became the family I longed for in my daydreams. What fun we all had, getting out of class and spending time doing something many of us loved to do.

The mural stood for a good thirty years, adorning the wall of that long hall until the school building was sold to become an office building. At that time, I was told, the history of civilization was erased forever—except from my heart.

The Standing Meditation

Preparation:

- Give thanks for the positive, calm mind tool of meditation.

- Select a quiet place indoors or in a garden.

- Bare your feet.

- Wear loose-fitting, cool clothing.

- Call to mind a sound that you may use to focus your thoughts. Any one-syllable sound is appropriate.

- Close your eyes and practice the sound you have chosen.

- Stand erect with your feet apart and even with your shoulders.

- Hang your arms at your sides or bend your arms and put your fingertips together to form a steeple. Next place them in front of your heart. I find this works better than hanging my arms.

- The focus of your meditation is relieving boredom and tension.

- When all is prepared, begin the meditation.

Begin the meditation

- Close your eyes.

- Use your one-syllable sound to clear every thought from your mind, and make sure that when you perform the sound that it is resonating intention, sounding strong and vibrant.

- You must mean business when you are clearing your mind of the tension or boredom of the day, because tension gets down into every muscle and tendon of your body.

- Now is the time to check your body for tension. If you carry your muscle tightness in your neck, try a few of the following neck exercises: Look straight ahead, take a few long, deep breaths, and on the exhale of the third one, slowly move your head as far as it will painlessly go to the left side. Hold that pose and inhale. On the exhale, slowly return your head to the forward position. Repeat with the right side. Remember only to move your head on the exhale. Repeat as many times as you must until the muscles relax, then continue with the meditation. If you hold your tension in the middle or lower back, stand erect and slowly lower your body, bending at the waist. Let your arms hang loosely in front and to the sides of your body. Do not bounce up and down; just relax your body in this position. This exercise will relieve the tension in the back, arms and buttocks. Breathe slowly in and out. After a moment or two, stand erect. If you still experience tight muscles somewhere in your body, repeat the procedure. Take your time, you are in no hurry.

- Be aware of your body. You are standing upright, supported by a skeleton that reaches the length of your spine, down your legs, and out your arms.

- Turn your attention to your feet. Imagine they are growing roots into the ground to further support your body.

- You are strong and becoming more so now that you are rooted into the ground.

- The roots grow deep and will not let you fall no matter how strong the wind or gale.

- You may stand in your awareness of your strength for as long as you wish. Bathe in that strength. Make it a part of your being.

- Know that you will only bend in the wind, not splinter and break.

- Realize that no matter the level of boredom, you will only bend in response to its resulting tension.

- Contemplate the strength of your body. Stand tall and deliberate.

- You are rooted in that strength that will forever sustain you, for you are wonderfully made of the clay in which you stand. It is part of you and you are part of it.

- When you are ready, imagine gently lifting one foot and then the other from the soft, cool ground.

- In your mind, retain the strength that you have garnered from this exercise.

- Remember the soothing feeling of your bare feet on the cool soil, and walk forward into consciousness.

- Take a deep breath and open your eyes.

Afterthought

I would wager that you thought you had not meditated at an early age or that you were told, like I was, that you were daydreaming and believed it. There is the chance that you had meditated. You may have focused your mind to a place where the conscious mind was not welcome, a place that may have brought you out of your boredom and stress to a place of happiness and peace, if only for a little while. In the story, I was delivered from the stigma of being a fish out of water by my teacher and my principal. In my adult world, this would not have happened; therefore, I have given you the adult version of the tension-buster meditation. I do hope that it was written with the clarity that you require.

Until I wrote this story down, I was not cognizant of the fact that my set intention for being part of a bunch of happy and fun-loving children had come to pass in my conscious life. It was an unexpected by-product of painting the history of civilization mural.

The standing meditation above demonstrates strength in all things. Circumstances may be out of your control, but they do not matter. You are rooted in the strength of your meditation. What you decide to do within that set of circumstances is the important lesson here. Stay calmly in the afterglow of the meditation while you decide how you will handle the situation that brought you to this meditation. It may have been a competitive spirit that has brought you to this place, or the boredom of being in a place where you do not want to be, as was my situation. In any case, your decisions will be well thought out and you will be ready for the realization of them.

Remember that you are not rooted inevitably in the situation that you are in. You do not have to be part of it, but you may choose to be. In that event, you may wish to use this meditation daily until you discern a better way to balance your feelings within your particular situation. I wish you peace on your journey to an unfettered reality.

Chapter 4

A Real Sewing Class

One at a time my grown daughters advised me of their wedding plans. My youngest would be married on June 15th. Would I please make her gown and headpiece for the wedding? Furthermore, there were four attendants who would also require gowns and headpieces.

My middle daughter came to me and advised me of her plans to be married on June 22 of the same year. Would I please make her wedding gown and a gown for her bridesmaid, who was, more or less, "Goth"? We would be covering some handmade tattoos for her—and oh yes, would I make the headpieces?

It was the year of 1985, a rather busy year I must admit, but I was not complaining. I was thrilled with the idea that they asked me to be such a large part of their collective weddings. And then I sat down to better focus on my prior experience in the field of sewing. It was a worrisome look back, at best.

In ninth grade home economics class, I had made a handkerchief apron. It consisted of one complete handkerchief for the center of the apron and a second one, cut diagonally, for either side of it. I finished it with a yard of grosgrain ribbon, cut in two and sewn on either side of the apron for ties. I received a C for the project.

In tenth grade, Mother bought me a piece of soft plaid wool for my sewing project and because a note from my teacher, Mrs. Rune, had clearly specified a plain-color piece of wool for the skirt I was about to make for myself, I was on my own. I matched the plaid as best I could and received a C on my report card.

Sewing was clearly not my thing, and since my father expected all A's from his eldest daughter, when I had the chance in eleventh grade to switch to photo shop, I did so. I received an A+ for the semester.

Looking forward was no better. I had no sewing machine, no money for material, was working overtime, did not use credit cards, and could not look to a bank for loans since I had no credit history.

This is a situation ripe for intercession. Prayer and meditation have always been my first line of defense, and this time, my focus was on ideas to make more money or to make the money I already earned stretch further.

In a few short hours, the answers came to mind, and they were interesting. My children were going to think I had gone round the bend and that they would have to look elsewhere for their gowns. Although I felt that the remedies to my concerns were a bit bizarre, I had nearly always trusted them in the past, and I would continue to do that. The solutions to this situation were threefold.

First I would sell my VW Beetle in order to purchase a sewing machine. My middle daughter happily sold the car to a friend of hers and I bought a top-of-the-line Singer 2000 with the proceeds.

Emboldened by the success of the first venture, I applied for a line of credit from the credit union near my place of employment. In a few days, to my amazement, the loan was approved and I had the required amount of money for my project.

With enough money in my purse to buy material for the first five gowns, my youngest daughter and I went shopping for a basic pattern and enough white satin and lace for the bride's attire. I added to that yards and yards of pink satin for the bridesmaids' dresses. I was a happy woman as I left the fabric shop.

The final part of my plan was to learn how to operate the sewing machine. I must have gained some brain cells since high school, since I had no problem learning the intricacies of the Singer 2000. In the two hours of study that I allotted myself to self-instruction, I learned how to use the sewing machine to the optimum. I was ready to begin.

I prepared the basic gown pattern for the wedding dress by pressing it with a dry iron, and reminded myself of a few cardinal rules concerning the placement of it on the satin material. I positioned the largest pattern pieces on the material first with the arrow printed on the pattern on the straight weave of the satin. Then I placed the smaller detail pieces on the material in the same manner. I cut and pinned the pattern tissue where my original sketches indicated the basic pattern should be supplemented. My design transformed the pattern for the gown, and I was ready to perform the scariest part of the process.

I sat down and composed myself before I took up the large dressmaking shears in my right hand. I remembered to cut the perimeter of the pattern, leaving a three-quarter inch seam allowance, and began to cut. If ever I were required to focus on the now, this would be the time to ask it of myself. I didn't have the money to buy additional yardage.

An hour later, I placed the shears back in the wooden box where I stored them. With a deep breath of relief, I sat down and prayed my thanks. I was on my way to a successful sewing project.

I connected the snowy pieces of fabric together in correct sequence, using the instruction that came with the basic pattern and finished the wedding gown with a soft, white cotton lining. The interesting details of the dress were saved for last. Fear made me put off those things I was not sure of, but now it was time to execute the tiny, white, satin-covered buttons and the corresponding wee little loops. I hand stitched them to the gown. There were about thirty of each, buttons and loops, marching hand and hand down the back of the dress. When the gown was complete, I hung it on a padded hanger with the buttons outward so I could admire them while I finished the veil. The lacy mantilla studded with seed pearls and a short pair of white lace gloves transformed the simple ensemble into one fit for a princess.

Once I began sewing, I found that I actually enjoyed the process, and the pink satin gowns were completed in a few weeks.

A second trip to the credit union allowed me another visit to the fabric store, in order to buy pale lavender faille and yards of white lace to overlay it for the second bride-to-be. I added to the yardage enough of the lavender faille to make the maid-of-honor's dress and began the process of making gowns for the second wedding.

This was to be a simply elegant wedding in a much larger church. The design of the gown would be substantial, but I did not realize how substantial I had constructed it until my daughter, halfway through the wedding reception, remarked how tired she was of holding it up.

Wearing a halo of flowers and a simple veil, and with lace-gloved hands holding a trembling bouquet, she floated toward the altar. Her attendant dutifully wore the gown I had designed for her, announcing that she would be removing it before the reception. But for some reason, within a few minutes of putting it on, she decided that she liked it. I heard that she wore the dress to bed that night.

Was the answer to that desperate and harried meditation, alternately prayed and beseeched, of great value to me? Of course it was. Did I miss my vehicle or have trouble paying the loan? Not as much as I would have thought. That single meditation gave me the strength of purpose to continue on and successfully finish this project.

Reaching my goal was amazing, and I will never forget the feeling I had when my daughters wore my creations on one of the happiest days of their lives. Thank you, my sweet daughters, for the experience.

The Walking Meditation

Preparation:

- Pray that the advice and instruction you receive during the meditation will be only for your good and for the good of others.

- Seek out a *safe* place to walk. During the meditation, you will likely not be as aware of your surroundings as you usually are.

- Make sure the route is relatively level.

- Try walking it before you begin the meditation.

- Wear soft shoes or slippers. You may walk barefooted if the terrain lends itself to that.

- Your clothes should be cool and comfortable.

- Your focus is a far-off mountain.

- Your subject for meditation is your ability to support yourself financially.

- Begin walking.

Begin the meditation

- Look far off into the distance and squint your eyes so that your surroundings do not distract from your meditation.

- Your subject today is your ability to support yourself in a meaningful way.

- You will focus on a faraway mountaintop and you will send yourself there in your subconscious. Visualize the mountain and your place on it, until you feel the rocky soil beneath you feet. Your conscious mind will try to distract you, but always return to the vision of the mountaintop.

- When you arrive on the mountain, sit down on a large rock to rest and contemplate.

- Bring to mind the reason you have brought yourself to this place in your mind.

- Request ideas to help you in your search for a way to support yourself and at least one other person.

- This part of the meditation may take hours or minutes. It is your choice. You are in no hurry.

- You may receive advice that you know in your heart you will not follow. If this happens, give thanks and walk back down the mountain. When you feel your feet on level ground, open your eyes.

- You may try another day to get advice that is acceptable to you.

- If the advice you receive resonates with you and you feel that you are able to accomplish what you have been advised to do, write it down in your subconscious mind. That way you will remember it. Your conscious mind will review and act upon it when the meditation is completed.

- When you are rested and ready, walk down the mountain path to level ground.

- Slowly open your eyes.

- Write down the advice you received in the meditation and follow it carefully. You may return to the meditation again for clarification any time you wish.

Afterthought

If you are at all creative, please do not expect mundane answers for your questions from your subconscious. Your answers may seem bizarre or outlandish, but check them out before you simply toss them away.

When I asked for a simple solution to the question about money, I was not really surprised that the answer seemed out of the ordinary because my subconscious mind has a predilection toward the strange and unusual. That is one of the main reasons I meditate. It is exciting to see what I come up with next!

There is no need to obey all the advice you receive in meditation, or any of it, for that matter. But, make sure you cannot adapt the advice to your own use before you decide on a solution from your conscious mind.

My daughters have rolled their eyes at some of the advice I have been given and have followed through with. But, as in the story above, the advice worked, and they paraded down their respective aisles, clothed and beautiful.

As you gain experience in meditation, you will learn to discern between the positive and the negative influences that advise you. You will always choose the positive, and if the advice is not clear, return to the meditation for clarification. It will be given to you.

Chapter 5

I Am Not Nervous!

Beginning as a teenager and on into adulthood, I have been driven into meditation prior to each time I had to speak in front of an audience. It could be as a teacher of a Sunday school class, a preacher of sermons, or as a gardener giving a presentation to the garden club. It did not matter—any time I had to speak publicly, I needed to meditate.

I had been admonished by my English teacher after passing out in front of the class; by my pastor, who told me that I lacked faith in God because I had a case of nerves prior to speaking for him; by my husband, who dismissively told me to "get over it;" and by my friends, who were very afraid that they would not be able to push me onto the stage for an important play I was involved in. But, I refused to be relegated to the rest of the crowd of defeated orators. I did not covet the moniker, "defeated," but sometimes I felt that I deserved it. Those were the times when I turned to meditation to treat this problem.

I have many stories I could tell you concerning speakers, their perceptions, and their realities. This story is a sad example of a speech gone wrong. When I was in eighth grade, one student in my class woke up to find that she was lying in a heap on the tile floor of the classroom. She had a goose egg sized bump on the back of her head from hitting the chalk tray on the way down to a dead faint.

The last she remembered, she was telling a funny story. Then the next thing she knew, she was picking herself up off the floor, and the teacher was asking for everyone to stand back in a tone suggesting that the poor girl may be rabid.

The nurse came running with her miniature doctor's bag at the request of a classmate, who had run down the hall with the news of another "fallen soldier." We seemed to be a class of fainters. We fell off the risers while singing in our spring concert gowns, rolled off the bleachers at band concerts, and in general had not missed a chance to lay outstretched on the floor at an event. It was never a question of *whether* someone would faint, but *when*?

Maybe the following story resonates with you. A young woman sat in a puddle of cold perspiration at an awards ceremony. She prayed not to win a prize she had worked extremely hard for all year, because then she would be required to speak in front of everyone. Of course, she had her speech in her hand, but the ink had run from the perspiration on it and she was unable to read it.

This is a classic: A mature woman had practiced a rather emotional and heartfelt thank-you speech in front of a mirror for two weeks. When the time came for her to speak, she walked hesitantly to the front of the room as if she had forgotten how to walk, delivered an embarrassed, "Thank you," and ducked out a side exit in order to save face.

As you may have guessed, all of those examples were experiences of mine. For years, my two personal best attempts at public speaking constituted playing with my hair with a pointer instead of actually pointing at something with it, and not speaking directly into a microphone. This trick left the audience leaning forward in their seats, straining to discover meaning in the undulating sounds and disembodied words coming from the PA system.

I am sure most of us have similar anecdotes lurking in the far regions of our mental closets. In fact, my friend Taylor says he takes off his shoes when he speaks before an audience, using as his reason that he feels more grounded when he does so. I do not believe that excuse for a moment. I think that he runs faster in bare feet!

Well, enough of that. Where do we go from here, in our search for a calm place from which we may perform our public speeches?

Perhaps you will travel to that subconscious place where all is calm and all questions are answered in order to make peace with speechmaking. You will return to consciousness having done that once and for all. I congratulate you. But many, like me, are required to revisit that calm place in our subconscious every time we get up to speak. But we are a tenacious bunch, are we not? We refuse to fail.

The Standing Meditation

Preparation:

- Pray that all negativity be erased from your conscious mind and be replaced with positivity.

- Cleanse the room in which you will be meditating. You may do this by washing the floors and walls with pine oil and warm water, or by lighting a bundle of dried sage and smoking the corners and crevices of the room. I would warn you here that the sage smells very much like marijuana, so you may want to perform the former cleanse.

- Remove extraneous objects from the room. A bare floor is much preferred to a carpeted one.

- Make sure you are wearing loose-fitting garments and that your feet are freshly washed. You will do this meditation in bare feet.

- Meditate on the speech at hand which you are scheduled to make.

- Stand in the place you wish to meditate. Do you feel comfortable in it? If you do not feel comfortable in the place, move around the room until you find the ideal place for you to begin.

- Lower the blinds, close the drapes, and use only a candle for light.

- Your point of focus is the intonation of sound "Om." This is a deep, reverberating sound that, when practiced, floats on the breath of the person "singing" it. The toning of Om and its respondent vibration carries far; replacing conscious thought and leaving the gate wide open for meditation.

Begin the meditation

- Intone the focus sound, Om. Within a few moments you will be in the meditation where all is calm.

- Be aware of each part of your body. Begin at the top of your head and move to your face. Notice your nose and eyes. Observe them from a vantage point inside your subconscious.

- Be mindful of your mouth and your ears. Survey the usefulness of them.

- Move down your spine to your shoulders. Take note of the strength in them.

- Your arms and hands are relaxed and in place at your sides.

- Journey upward to your chest and down to the life center of your body, your navel.

- Observe your amazingly constructed reproductive organs and give thanks for them, for through them comes new life.

- Move on to focus on your thighs and knees. See them at attention, for they assist your body to stand upright.

- Finally, move to your calves, ankles, and feet.

- Feel the meeting of your feet and the bare wood of the floor.

- Imagine the soles of your feet becoming one with the wood of the floor. You cannot fall, for you are strong in your construction and immoveable in fearful circumstances.

- Your body benefits from the strength of emotion. Therefore, observe yourself as you move inward for additional strength and for wisdom. Ask for the wisdom, and know that it will be given to you.

- Call up an image of yourself giving the most professional speech of your life. You are relaxed, witty, and intelligent. You know your subject well. Your clothes show impeccable taste, and your audience is enraptured under your spell.

- Enjoy the image that you see there. Meditate as long as you wish, for to see this image of yourself as a competent speaker fills your heart with joy.

- Ask that the image become your truth and know that it will.

- When you are sated with joy, photograph that image. You will want to keep it with you, to copy it onto your conscious mind as you slowly come to the end of the meditation. You know that the photograph of you as a respected speaker will go with you in your conscious mind and prompt you, reminding you of this meditation every time you have need of it.

- You will see a door ahead of you. Stand at that door and knock.

- As the door opens for you, open your eyes.

Afterthought

I am reminded of the story in the book of Exodus, Chapter 4, in which Moses was asked by God to do a little public speaking. God showed him how to do some miracles, as visual aids, for the Israelites he would address. But, do you think Moses was grateful? Do you think he said, "Okay, I will go right this minute and speak to the sons and daughters of Abraham about you?"

Oh no, Moses cried that he had never been eloquent and that he was slow of speech and could not possibly speak in public. God was very patient with him and tried to change Moses' mind. He asked Moses just who he thought gave him speech in the first place. And God further assured Moses that he would teach him the words to say.

Moses continued to moan, groan, and complain, and he finally had the nerve to ask God—who was speaking from the burning bush, no less—to send someone else instead of him. And God did.

He selected Moses' brother, Aaron, to do the job. God had not let Moses off the hook entirely, but insisted that he still perform the miracles that God had shown him. I do not know how Moses got off so easily. I know for sure that those who have asked me to speak never took no for an answer!

I related the story about Moses to illustrate that you are in good company when you try to beg off when asked to speak publicly. But, do not expect the gentle persuasion or the loving kindness exhibited by God to be the norm, for sadly, it is not.

I have come to the conclusion that there is absolutely no reason for the fear a public speaker inflicts upon him or herself. Your ego simply feels the need to be in control of you in your speech-making. Your ego would tell you that your dress is too long, your heels too high, your tie is the wrong color, or anything else that could take you off course and not let you be who you are.

This egomaniac is part of you and must be brought under control. I know it is easy for me to say, for in reality, it takes effort and more patience than you may think you have to make your mind believe what your heart already knows.

Your heart knows that it is only the body, not the spirit, trembling before a waiting crowd—a crowd that has more confidence in you than you have in yourself. Therefore, tell your ego to take a back seat. It is not in charge of you, you are—and mean it every time you say it.

I know that you will take the photographic vision of yourself as a successful speaker from the meditation as your truth. And if you ever need reminding of that truth, you will go back to the meditation for a refresher course. You will find, as I have, that the trips back to this meditation become rarer as you become more confident in yourself. Be at peace.

Chapter 6

Luna Number Two

Luna is that part of me that is in constant touch with my subconscious. She is the real deal, knows the truth about me, and serves as my Dutch uncle. Luna has no compunction about telling me where I am missing the mark in life and what I should do about it. She was and still is my muse. I have been a painter since I was ten and when Luna began visiting my meditations early in 2004, her physical appearance was so striking that from my experience painting the human figure, I decided to make her a model for a series of paintings which were in the planning stage.

My framer called one early spring morning in 2006, to request a painting. She was in charge of twisting the arms of artists that she knew for a donation of a painting to auction in benefit of one of my favorite charities, a women's and children's shelter nearby.

I told her that I would come up with something and that I would get back to her on the subject. I surveyed my inventory of paintings but found no painting that I thought was suitable for this sale. I decided to paint my new vision especially for this important event. In the next few days, Luna and her glorious physique came to mind again and again, as I used Automatic writing as a tool for my choice of a subject to paint. I finally decided to paint Luna's portrait for the benefit show. I painted a full-body portrait of her, developed in the abstract, and I could barely contain my joy at the peace that radiated from that canvas. Could I submit it to the auction or would I elect to give a lesser quality piece in its place? It was a fleeting thought and I submitted Luna's portrait as I had promised myself I would.

The morning of the auction, I arrived at the mansion in Lebanon, Pennsylvania, to find my painting of Luna displayed smack in the middle of a sea of flower paintings. She made quite a focal point. As I seated myself in the garden among the artists and bidders, I was undecided whether to pray for a sale or to pray that the bidders wanted only paintings of flowers. I knew the right thing to do, but I was very attached to that painting. At the end of the bidding, Luna sold for a reasonable sum of money and was whisked away by the buyer, an interior decorator, before I could say goodbye to her.

I felt it was important for me to begin painting another version of Luna as soon as possible. I missed the first painting and needed to get on with the series. I made the decision to start painting immediately.

The next morning I began the process to paint Luna. I wrestled a large, newly sized canvas from the studio to the sunroom. I had already assembled the acrylic paints and the properly large brushes needed to paint such a large canvas. All that was left to do was to prepare a bit of water and a dinner-sized plate to use as a palette.

I squeezed a large blob of titanium white and smaller globs of Cadmium Yellow, Raw Sienna, and Hooker's Green onto the plate. I chose a four-inch flat brush from my handful of large brushes, dampened it, and began painting.

As I laid in the colors, I noticed that this portrait, Luna Number Two, came into being as a less amoebic form than the original Luna portrait which I had painted a few months before. It took on more of the lines and curvy aspects one sees in the human form. This part of me, this Luna Number Two, became the vision in my meditations.

With much emotion, I carefully filled in the basic structure of the composition, not bothering with outlines at this point in the process. I had planned to apply light and near-white hues to the background of the painting, but I found that I had instead dipped my brush into the green and yellow ones, which I had reserved for the draping of Luna's lower body.

The subject herself guided me to a grittier palette. The painting was not to be light and airy, but dark and solemn. In the end I deferred to those new creative instincts, letting them overrule what I had originally planned. I painted quickly and surely, as if I knew exactly where I was going with her portrait.

After a few hours of work, I stood back to look at what I had painted. The power of it stunned me. It was not at all what I had anticipated. Viewing the portrait in a full-length mirror fooled the deficiencies I experience with my eyesight, and I calmed myself by contemplating the mirrored strength of this painting.

I had to ask myself two questions at this juncture of the painting process: could my literal mind have done better? And, could I have painted a more commanding, yet love-filled and emotional portrait? The answers were no and no, for I could not have painted this stunning painting with my conscious mind alone.

The rusty brown of Luna's back, neck, and arms defied a color name but looked completely rational in the context of this composition. The colors for the drape across her body were used for the background of her portrait, compelling me to mix a new and different one.

This new color on my palette was required to be the darkest color on the canvas in order to ground the painting. Not satisfied with any of my mixtures and in frustration, I combined the rust, green, and yellow—the leftover colors that I had previously applied to the canvas—with a tablespoon of Payne's Gray. With the perfect color finally discovered, my work continued with the painting of the drape on Luna's lower body.

When I felt the portrait of Luna was near completion, I stood back a few feet to look at it. Then, as usual, I asked my subconscious for assistance in completing the painting.

Usually when I did this a change would come to mind, one in either color or form. Once in a while, I was told to put the painting in the studio to bring out another day for evaluation. That day, I was given one word, and it was *integrated*. I had not a clue what that word meant in the context of the portrait of Luna.

I considered the word *integrated*, and after a few hours, a thought came to mind concerning Integrated Circuit Cards. I still had no idea why I must include them in the painting, but it was becoming more and more urgent to me that I do so. I decided to sleep on the problem, and if I had no solution to my situation the next day, I would return to the meditation and request clarification of this ICC business.

That night, what came to me in a dream saddened me. I was shown a situation that I had consciously refused to address for many years. The parental abuse, the beatings, the hurtful, hateful words that were spit at me, had all contributed to my broken and disembodied spirit. And the divided mind and heart that I knew would someday push itself to the surface had done so with this emotional painting of Luna. This time, the subject would not go away unaddressed. The fractured parts of my psyche would require restoration, and that restoration would be in the form of an unorthodox creation, the second version of Luna.

The next morning before drinking my coffee, I went to the closet in my studio. There was the chest where I had stored circuit cards that were gleaned from some unusable telephones. I do not know why I had saved them and stored them in the chest. I only knew that I required them for this portrait.

I carried the ICCs to the worktable where Luna lay drying and closed my eyes before I requested the directions for their placement on the painting. When I reopened my eyes, I took up the circuit cards from the box and, one by one, positioned them on the rusty spine in the image. I arranged them and rearranged them until I felt they were in the correct positions.

In the end, those clusters of circuit cards became symbols of the parts of me that had become disconnected. They were the pieces of my heart and mind that required integration. Stepping back from the portrait, I noticed that each cluster of ICCs was affixed over a nerve center. I took a deep and powerful breath and felt the peace that always accompanies wholeness of mind and spirit.

Through the creative and meditative work that I had named Luna Number Two, I had lovingly and prayerfully helped heal my broken self. I had come out the other side ensured that I was, indeed, integrated.

I know of many creative people—artists, musicians, and writers—who have described the deep and transformative changes that have taken place in their lives as they created their works. I listened and I believed them then, but only now did I truly understand.

The Sitting Meditation

Preparation:

- Thank God for the creative part of your brain that accepts His will in all things.

- Choose a straight-backed chair. Sit in it and make sure you are comfortable. An uncomfortable seat may take your focus to a place of pain instead of calm.

- Dim the lights to a setting that does not create glare for your eyes.

- Ensure that the clothes you are wearing are soft and nonbinding, especially around the waist.

- Make plain, in your conscious mind, the outcome you wish from the meditation.

- Settle on an organic item to use as your focus point for this meditation. I am partial to river rock, because of its properties. It has been worn smooth by ages of water flow. In other words, it has a history. You may opt for a reed of some type that personifies your willingness to be influenced by God or an artifact of your own choosing. Whatever you decide on, the idea for your focus will be the right one for you.

- Hold the river rock or other focus object in your hand. Imagine how it may have been born. Was it sharp and jagged, ready for the polishing of the cool, clean water? Was your chosen object once only partly formed until nature slowly shaped it into the form it has today?

- Think of yourself as that object, and when you succeed in that thought and thinking no other one, you are ready to begin.

Begin the meditation

- Sit in the chair that you chose. Place your feet flat on the floor. Make sure you are comfortable.

- Close your eyes and drift to a faraway place.

- You are the jagged rock. You are the object not yet fully formed. You lie in the soft silt of the river bottom and wait, with great anticipation, for the flow of the river; you are the artifact spread atop the mesa to wait for the scouring of the wind.

- Choose that part of you that you consider jagged, sharp, or not fully polished (your mind or your body, for instance). Take as much time as you require to fully research this in your mind. You are not in a hurry.

- Consider the reason for your selection. For the purpose of this exercise, you chose your body. It was that your mouth was out of control. Remember to take the time to reflect on this subject.

- Reason how the mind affects the words that come out of your mouth. Bring any religious or secular teachings that you have been taught into the mix, if you wish, to assist in the concentration of your thoughts and allow you to reach your logical conclusion.

- At this point, allow the cool water to wash over you. In your mind, allow the water to flow over you again and again until you are smooth. Let the wind do its marvelous work on you until your body and mind are one.

- Realize that the flow of water over the rock is allowed by the rock. The wind is allowed by the artifact.

- Know that it is so with you, as well. You allow the Source of your being to guide you in your conscious life as well as your subconscious life in order for you to be polished and smooth.

- Grasp the stone tightly in your hand or take your chosen artifact in your grasp, realizing that it is a metaphor for the guided life.

- You are no longer the object. You hold the object. Your fully formed artifact in turn, holds the remembrance of the wisdom in this meditation.

- When you are ready, completely open your eyes.

- Slip your chosen object into your pocket.

- As your day fades into night, you will put your hand in your pocket, perhaps a dozen times, to feel the object and remember the wisdom of the meditation.

Afterthought

The story above is a true one and illustrates what happens when you are attuned to God's will. It illustrates that when you trust Him, and are sure that He never guides you down an alternate path without reason, your life will flow more smoothly. Your Source has a vested interest in keeping you on the straight and narrow path that leads to Him.

In the sitting meditation, you give thanks for your talents and for the use of them in healing your life. I used the analogy of the jagged rock—that when it gives permission to the water to wear it and hone it, it becomes beautiful and smooth and the artifact, that when it gives permission to the wind it is scoured to an unnatural beauty, and it becomes an adornment. But I will stress here that you must give permission for this to happen. I have found that the river rock or an artifact such as a raw turquoise are great focus pieces for this meditation and can be kept as long as you wish to remember the wisdom in a valuable meditation.

The preceding meditation looks deceptively simple. It is not. There is a deeper level of concentration to be had, where there are pregnant pauses in the instruction. I have provided those pauses to you so that you may experience a deeper understanding of the meditation.

In previous meditations, I have been feeding you milk from a bottle. In this one I have added the fruit and vegetables. My wish is that you have benefited from the meal.

Chapter 7

The Vacuum Cleaner

I have been careful, since I no longer drive, to situate myself in small towns in whatever area I have decided to reside. This way, I assured myself of having access to everything I needed, and I would have it no other way.

Millerston is one such typical small town that I clearly recall. It was my home for a few years in the late nineties. It had its share of churches and banks, lodge halls and pharmacies. There were doctors who practiced there and did not think it out of the ordinary when a patient requested he visit them, and dentists who would open up the office on Sunday if you happened to break a tooth on a hard pretzel while watching the game. It was a great little town, and that was where I met Poor Mildred.

A small group of us got together with like-minded people once a month. We had teas and picnics in the summer and holiday parties and movie nights in the winter. All of these activities included Poor Mildred.

Mildred was a lovely lady, really, but our perception was that she had a glaring problem. Even though small town dwellers are famous for gossiping, she took the talent for it to a new level, leading some of her oldest friends to lovingly nickname her The Vacuum Cleaner—because she picked up all the dirt!

We tried to tell Poor Mildred (We always thought of her as Poor Mildred) that perhaps the gossiping was a bit overdone. We included ourselves in this, since we did not want to hurt her feelings. Well, she did not take hints very well. She listened politely, with a blank face, until we completed our hint, and then, without missing a beat, continued her gossiping. Gossip seemed to be the oxygen that Poor Mildred breathed and the stamina-producing food that she needed to chew on daily. It was the social outlet that gave her importance.

One morning in early spring, we noticed that Poor Mildred was not at her station on her front porch. She was not leaning over the railing, gossiping, which was her usual routine. In fact, her front door was closed, her drapes were pulled, and the cottage seemed deserted.

By midday, we grew concerned that she had fallen ill or that there had been a death in the family. Although there were visitors to her front door, it was not opened for any of them. When we phoned, no one answered.

This continued throughout the day until Poor Mildred's husband arrived home from his job as a car salesman. Instead of parking his new car in front of his house as a form of advertisement as usual, he parked it on the side street closest to his back door. He jumped out of his vehicle and walked quickly across the side yard. This was a curious thing for him to do, seeing as he had posted "keep off the grass" signs on three sides of his flawless lawn. He looked no other way but straight ahead as he approached his back door, entered, and slammed it closed.

We were heartbroken. A tragedy had obviously occurred and we, Poor Mildred's best friends, were precluded from helping her. We reminded each other not to be creative in our speaking, for we really had no facts on which to base a probable story. But, each of us coveted the chance to be of help. The niggling was in the back of every mind, requiring knowledge of her problem. We tried to busy ourselves with projects that had nothing to do with her, but the fact was our thoughts gravitated to Poor Mildred daily.

One day a few months after Poor Mildred went into hiding; her only daughter came to visit, with her fiancé in tow. They were holding hands and talking animatedly to each other as they walked up the pavement, across the porch, and entered the front door. Problem solved. Mildred's daughter was obviously pregnant. We were relieved that a baby was coming, and we later learned that the two of them were married quietly that day, by their pastor. Unfortunately, Mildred and her husband declined to attend.

Mildred's friends and neighbors sincerely tried not to judge her, but we never again thought of her as "Poor Mildred." The dynamics of our separate relationships had shifted, and the closeness had eroded.

A few short months later, Mildred came out of hiding. She acknowledged us when we happened to meet, but the friendliness that was once her hallmark had faded. She did not explain the reason for her self-imposed withdrawal from society, because she perceived that we knew the reason.

In fact, when she had anything of substance to say to us, it was to accuse her friends and neighbors of gossiping about her. But for once, she was wrong. We had nothing to gossip about. Then one day, she said something very revealing to one of her oldest friends. Mildred felt that she had been the topic of our conversation, for she certainly would have engaged in the gossip.

In the end, I deduced by her words and actions that our neighbor had taken a cold and lonely look inward at her life during the time she was sequestered in the tiny cottage. And, she had found feelings of humiliation and sorrow there. Although some of us are fond of saying, "What goes around comes around," we could not even think of applying the phrase to Mildred.

As time went on, we found that Mildred deserved her amended name, for she created in herself a more positive way to interact with others. She served as a reminder to all of us that many times, all we need is some time alone to meditate and pray to straighten us out.

We only hoped that hints and tactful mentoring from our friends would not be ignored, and that we would not wait for a catastrophe to crash into our quiet lives before we righted ourselves. We have found, though, that even a perceived catastrophe can put us right back on the path where we belong. This perceived catastrophe was given the beautiful name of Lily Ann. She was named for her grandmother, and according to Mildred's daughter, Mildred took one look at her grandchild and fell in love.

The reconciliation that took place among mother, daughter, and grandmother was joyous and complete. In less than a year, negative perceptions were eased. Was there ongoing work to be done to keep their lives as positive and loving as possible? Of course there was, for there is not a perfect one among us here on earth.

The Sitting Meditation

Preparation:

- By this point in time, you may have preserved a clean, quiet place in which to meditate. Those three points above—preserved, clean, and quiet—are the first elements of your meditative process. They will serve you well.

- If you have a tape or CD of birdsong, it would be relevant to play it in the background for this meditation. If you do not have such a CD or tape, you will benefit from the absolute quiet.

- Choose an egg to hold in your hand as a reference or focus point.

- Prepare for yourself soft and comfortable clothes.

- Prepare your mind for the subject of this meditation. Discard thoughts that your ego has thrown in your path such as, what other people think of you or if you have been forgiven the errors you have made. Retain the positives such as your love for your neighbor and your intention to live your life peaceably.

- You may picture yourself putting the negatives in a trash bag, twisting it shut, taking it out to the edge of the universe, and pitching it into that dark blue vastness so that it will be transmuted into something positive.

- The subjects for this meditation are a letdown and the unforgiving spirit.

- If you have it playing, pay attention to the birdsong.

Begin the meditation

- Sit on a yoga block and cross your legs in front of you. This variation of the sitting meditation pose raises you off the floor and gives you a different perspective from which to begin. You may also use a blanket or cushion. Are you comfortable? If not, make it so.

- Place the egg you have chosen in your cupped hands and close your eyes.

- Hear the birdsong, or just the quietness around you. Listen as long as you like.

- Feel the oval egg in your hands. It is a symbol of life to you.

- Meditate on the new life that you would desire for yourself. This may take time, but you are not in a hurry.

- Taste the sweetness of a loving and giving spirit. If you cannot do this, ask yourself what is coming between you and the sweetness.

- If you taste, instead, the sourness of the unforgiving spirit, ask why it is so.

- For the purpose of this meditation, you will survey the perceptions of disappointment and forgiveness.

- Look at the dark cloud of disappointment. As it turns around in front of you, examine it closely from all sides.

- Decide how you will dismantle this dark cloud of disappointment, for if you do not, you cannot see or experience the love and joy that it obscures.

- You have perhaps decided that the part of the cloud closest in proximity to you, in the meditation, will be the first to take apart. It is labeled embarrassment.

- You realize that the complex reason for your embarrassment is not the pregnancy, or the error in judgment, whatever that may be, but it is knowing that you would have spread that news all over town, or felt elated at the thought of someone else in trouble, if it not been your daughter or son.

- The second part of that dark cloud is the hurt. You recognize that feeling hurt is a selfish emotion, and most people cannot stand to be called selfish, even when it is their subconscious shouting it. The hurt says that you have expended so much time and energy to your daughter, and look what she did with it! You have invested so much in your son's education, and now he refuses to get a job. Love says that everyone makes choices in life, and you wanted to do everything you did for your daughter or your son, and another part of the cloud dissipates as you begin focusing on your love for your daughter or your son.

- Thirdly, you discover that with the other two parts of the dark cloud erased only disappointment is left for you to look at and resolve. Now that you can clearly see the love you have always had for your daughter or son, even that final wisp of darkness fades away and you realize that forgiveness is staring you directly in the face. That final piece of the grayness that clouded your vision is lifted and you are able to forgive.

- Bring the birdsong back into your hearing. Enjoy it for as long as you wish.

- Feel the oval egg symbolizing your new life. It is cradled softly in your palms. You will nurture this new life, and if you perceive that you are returning to your old way of thinking, promise yourself that you will return to this meditation.

- When you are ready, open your eyes.

Afterthought

I address the art of forgiveness in many of my stories, for it is of great importance for you to forgive in this life. As a Christian, I know that the measure in which I forgive others, will forgiveness be meted to me. Your religion may also teach this concept, for it seems to be a universally accepted one. All that taken into account, it makes you feel right with the universe to forgive.

Remember to forgive others, and in the process, live your life free of this burden. Forgiveness for you is one of the best tools for freeing yourself, emotionally. So remember to give yourself the gift of forgiveness, and do not revisit that same hurtfulness ever again. Love yourself for the person you are, and realize that every day of your life is a good day for gift-giving. I send you love.

Chapter 8

Stacking Needles

Ellen became a member of my extended family, but only for a time. And before I ever met her, I was shown pictures and told stories of this beautiful and vivacious woman. I took all of these stories to be true. She was about fifty years old when I finally met her in the parking lot of a restaurant. She was approximately fifteen years my senior at the time.

I knew we had been invited to the same dinner, and I was very anxious to meet her. But when her husband, Lawrence, introduced Ellen to me, I was astonished by the look of her. Her demeanor was unmistakably bitter. The downturned corners of her mouth mirrored her down-sloping shoulders and the fist clenched at her right side. With her left hand she held her bag tightly to her solar plexus, as if she thought someone was about to snatch it from her. Her gray, unkempt hair was no surprise to me as I looked at the whole of her. She was not what I had expected.

She nodded her greeting as I managed to say hello to her. In response, she looked beyond me and I was tempted to look over my shoulder at her point of interest. I suddenly felt that I needed to know what event or series of events had transformed the charmingly beautiful woman of the snapshots I had been shown into this woman. As she stood uncertainly before me, I wanted to restore her to herself and remove the mask and the too-large, black clothes in which she had dressed herself. I wanted a lot, but what I got was a definite snub.

Jumping into the deep end, as usual, I linked my left arm into her rigid right one, ignoring the fist, and we advanced toward the door of the restaurant where we were about to dine.

Once inside, Lawrence graciously took her arm from mine and, grasping her elbow, guided her to the right of the head of the table. When he had politely seated her, he came back for me. He guided me down the long expanse of table.

There were twenty pairs of eyes staring at me as I passed each seated guest, until we finally reached the far left chair at the end of the table, near the kitchen. It was obvious that this restaurant was ill equipped for a banquet of this size, as the double doors to the kitchen bumped my chair when opened. It was of no consequence to me, because from this vantage point, I could plainly scrutinize the object of my attention.

The food was excellent, but I ate little of it. My eyes were riveted on Ellen. In my mind I continued my reconstruction of her to match the now with the then—my prior perception of what she was supposed to be like. After the meal, I was introduced to the guests that were new to me, and I said my good-byes to the host and hostess. Reluctantly, I walked out the door of the restaurant across the parking lot and got into my car. It was difficult for me to keep my mind on my driving as I headed for home.

I had no sooner arrived home when the phone rang. It was Lawrence. He invited me to his and Ellen's home the following Thursday evening for cocktails. I said I would be there. He countered with the statement that his secretary would call me with the details and hung up the phone.

This had been a jaw-dropping day for me, and exhausted as I was from it, my mind was still racing. Before I would allow myself to rest, I would meditate on the day and learn from those lessons it contained.

True to his promise, Lawrence's secretary called the following Monday morning to provide the time of our gathering and directions to their home.

Thursday evening came quickly enough, and as I carefully dressed myself and applied a bit of makeup, I pondered the wisdom of going to the trouble. I wondered if Ellen had done the same, transforming herself into the beauty she had been in the photos I'd seen. Although I wished it to be true, I held out little hope that it was.

I was greeted at the door by a lovely woman who took my coat for me, then ushered me into the great room. There I found Ellen, seated on a straight chair, holding her body rigid and clasping her hands together in her lap. There was no softness to her and no ladylike graces, such as crossing her legs. At that moment, I felt great pity for her.

Lawrence stood up from his high-backed chair to gesture me to the one assigned me. We were quiet for a moment, then, hating dead air, I told them how lovely it was that they had invited me to their home. There were two nods and more dead air as I took in the great room. It might have been very beautiful, if someone had cared to put in more effort to make it a home. The room was scrubbed spotless, as sterile-seeming as a lab, and just as chilly.

I turned to Ellen with a question concerning the dinner the previous Friday, and Lawrence answered it. Another false start to the conversation ended with a retort from him. Alright, I got it. He was her mouthpiece.

When I spoke directly to him, he ignored what I said and offered me a tour of their home. I was up for anything that would break the deadlock that had been our interaction for the last twenty minutes.

As I was shown from room to room, I noticed the same eerie un-lived-in appearance throughout. Their house was spacious and magnificently built, but you could not call it a home. Not by any stretch of the imagination was this house a place where friends and family could gather and be joyful.

That evening I continued my study of Ellen. The tense feeling of her house, the more-than-clean rooms with nothing out of place, caused me to notice that relevant pieces of her home life mirrored her public life. The extreme armoring of her body shouted the tenseness she must have felt. Her scrubbed but unadorned body showed the same mindset as the undecorated house in which she lived. But I needed to know more.

I soon became a de facto member of this family and was often asked to visit. Ellen became more comfortable with me as time passed, and it seemed to me that she might let her guard down and confide in me. That would be a great start on the road to trust and the restoration of friendships. I could only pray it to be true.

One day, Lawrence drove Ellen to my apartment to visit. It might have been the change of venue for our chats, but it seemed that she could not wait to tell me something. According to her, it had been on her mind since our first meeting and without warning unorganized information fairly gushed from her mouth. For awhile, I tried to focus on what she was telling me, but after a few minutes I was tempted to put my palms over my ears and do the "La, la" thing, but I restrained myself. After all, this was what I had been waiting for.

Picking out some relevant information that would be of use in helping Ellen was a challenge as there was no recording or taking notes of her rapid monologue, but I was willing to do my best. She had commented on disappointment, shame, murder and much more, as I tried to piece together the meaning of it all.

Ellen soon realized that she may have said something more than she intended to and abruptly ended her ranting. She immediately swore me to secrecy, which probably was not necessary, and I promised myself to remember only those things she said that would be of value to me in order to help her. At her insistence, I wrote down those items that she felt were the most grievous and signed off on them. She had instinctively known that she could talk to me and that I would try to help her if I could. At the time of her rant, she was reaching out for help, but as you read, she pulled back before any assistance could be offered to her.

Her story was one that I had heard many times as a Christian counselor. Lawrence had become attracted to a young, beautiful woman who came to work for his company in a temporary capacity. She, in turn, was friendly and outgoing in his presence, sometimes being a bit flirtatious. For one reason—or, I expect, many reasons—they fell in lust.

Ellen found out about the affair by way of an anonymous phone call, and when she presented the information to Lawrence, he became outraged. Was she not well taken care of? Did she not have enough of his money? Just what was the problem with her?

Since Lawrence refused to address the subject of the other woman, Ellen retreated, finding solace in showing him the results of his indiscretion—and show him she did. Her bitter demeanor and absolute disgust for him was more than apparent as she taunted him with the unspoken words, "Look what you did to me."

In time, Ellen turned to her Bible. She read it and interpreted it in her own inimitable way, convincing herself that Lawrence had committed murder, for he had unilaterally killed their marriage.

With my newfound knowledge of their problem, I tried to tell her of other couples who struggled over the hurdle of adultery and had, through work, love for each other, and their commitment to each other and God, reinvested in their marriages. For Ellen all of this went in one ear and out the other.

I invited Ellen and Lawrence to meet with some of those couples who had vowed to help others through this difficult situation. But Ellen would not give credence to any alternative beyond that of what she thought she had read in the Bible. Lawrence was a murderer.

Finally, I asked her to show me her source of reference in the Bible and offered that I thought perhaps she was putting her own spin on something she had read. She refused. Since I had come to my breaking point for the day, I left for home and my cat, Dorothy—who is quite sane, and a welcome change from what I had just experienced.

On so many levels, this situation distressed me. Ellen was negating that beautiful and vivacious woman she used to be because Lawrence had made a gross error in judgment. Why would she insist on doing that? Most women I know would take a good look at themselves to try figure out their part in all of it, go to counseling, or do *something*. Then if they could not make sense of it all and their spouses were just bad apples, they would leave the marriage. I was totally perplexed by Ellen's actions.

Lawrence, unrepentant, had decided to continue the affair, rubbing his wife's nose in the whole mess. Instead of Ellen taking the high road, she decided to do herself in, mentally.

Instead of the purse Ellen used to clutch to her belly, she now clutched the Bible. I told her as gently as possible that she may as well lay down the book, for all the reading in the world was of no use if you did not interpret it correctly, did not understand it, or glossed over the writings that you disagreed with. Furthermore, she was stacking needles and was bound to get stabbed over and over again. Why had she insisted on being hurt repeatedly?

I assumed that the last statement that I uttered would mean the end of the relationship, for I found that Ellen only tolerated people who agreed with her in what she was saying and doing. I had simply run out of suggestions to help her. I suspected that my ouster from her life had left her not one friend that loved her enough to say the things to her that needed to be said.

I prayed for Ellen and Lawrence, but I stayed away. I think it was Saint Paul who told us not to toss our pearls before swine. In other words, you can explain and teach the scriptures, but when your words are not heard, do not trouble yourself or your inattentive audience any further. Shake the dust from off your feet and walk away from the situation, he further stated, and that is just what I did.

The Walking Meditation

Preparation:

- Pray for clarity in all that you study and interpret.

- If you have a large yard or piece of land, you are in luck, but a few yards of level ground will surely suffice. Map out a circle for your walking meditation.

- You may make this circle permanent by putting down soft sand on the path.

- Choose a cross or another object that represents your faith, to use in this meditation.

- Decide on the subject of your meditation. If you need to reread the story to form some of your own ideas, please do that now.

- Remove your shoes.

- Wear soft, comfortable clothing.

- Ready your mind by using the universal Om.

- Begin walking with your eyes slightly open and looking straight ahead.

Begin the Meditation

- Continue toning the Om.

- Walk slowly on the path you have mapped out.

- Take up the cross or other focus object in your palm. Finger it as you would a talisman.

- Study the surface of the cross or the irregularities of your chosen object with your fingers so that you recognize it by touch.

- Search for clarity in your meditation concerning the source of your being. That force that makes you alive and strong. That one entity that causes you to feel strong emotions such as love and forgiveness. It may be your God or just a sense that you are not alone in the universe

- Spend as much time in consideration of your Source as you wish, for time will mean nothing to you as you study and reflect on the most important part of you, the person within.

- When you are clearly in tune with your Source or you are extremely fatigued in the consideration of it, you may wish to continue another day.

- Give thanks for your experience in the meditation.

- Look toward the light and walk out into it.

- Open your eyes.

Afterthought

The story of Ellen is a sad one, but one in which there are many positives. You may be able to see Ellen as the person she could have been, as I do, or you may see her as one you would rather not emulate. In either instance, there is at least one lesson here. You may want to choose a different meditation than this one. I chose this meditation because it was a lesson point that I wanted to share with you. There are four parts to this lesson. Each part is valuable to you as you study and meditate:

- Use prayer and meditation when you study important text.

- Keep excellent references by your side as you search for a clear lesson from your study.

- Consider the opinions of learned men and women who make sense to you.

- Remember that there is a time and place for strong emotions, but when you are seeking clarity is not the time, or the place.

  Insisting that a text agree with your preformed conclusions is not the best solution to your problems, and may create more discord than solace for you. Work out your problems carefully, secure in the knowledge that your clarity is there for the asking. I wish you success in your own various studies.

Chapter 9

Musing with My Muse

I was too old to continue. I was sure of it. My talents were in decline, and I was washed up.

Painting in the mode I had previously used no longer satisfied me. The brushstrokes were too broad and barren of meaning. My stories and parables no longer made sense to me or to anyone else, and my music had died as surely as in "American Pie." I felt that I was going down in flames.

I struggled to find meaning in my life as I was living it then, and found none. All that seemed left to me was to mourn my perceived losses, and I did. Then, one evening, Luna made an unexpected appearance in my meditation. She had come to give me a "fitness report."

Luna is my muse. She dwells in that part of my brain that creates, and she nourishes my soul. She has a long and slender body the color of a mesa at sunset and short red, tightly curled hair that turns golden in the aura light of my meditation. She is glorious to behold. My muse has a no-nonsense attitude and fancies that she is the boss of me. As she is a part of my subconscious, I agree to this treatment. I needed not guess why she turned up in this particular evening's meditation—I knew why.

No one else could set me straight like she could. She would dig deep into my soul to bring all the dirt to the surface for me to examine, and she had strong opinions on every grain of it. This time, Luna stood by my side as we looked at the results of her dig. One by one, she reflected on each of my negative perceptions. She knew that I did not get hints, and she guided me toward the clean-up of the wrong thinking that I had buried. Luna explained that negative perceptions which I had voluntarily pleated into my subconscious mind were causing my conscious meltdown. Our work, once more, would be to replace the negative with the positive.

Truth by truth, Luna wove together a collage that formed a patchwork of my talents. She introduced me to all my radical fears and then she concealed them all with the quilt of truth she had constructed. I was admonished not to lift the corners of that covering by reinstating the negative thoughts I had been expressing.

Luna had a plan to assist me further. She strongly suggested that I create a break between projects. I would paint for a scheduled length of time and do the same for both writing books and music. No longer would I hurdle from one discipline to another. One project must be completed before another began. Ignoring my protests to her plan, she forged valiantly ahead to the real reason she had appeared in my meditation.

According to Luna, the lesson I was required to learn was this: never again would I slap God in the face by quitting those talents that he had graciously bestowed on me. (I told you that she was tough).

When the meditation ended and my muse departed my field of vision, my face burned in shame and I wiped away the tears that inevitably accompanied her visits. I have not executed Luna's plan to the letter, for at this moment I am writing this book and a piece of music is roaring in my mind, waiting to be written down. And I am working out, in my mind, the problems inherent in any portrait that I attempt to paint, especially a half-finished one owed to a family member.

Luna has continued to instruct me in the ways of my Source and I have continued to listen, but not always to obey. Her latest instruction was for me not to diminish my talents to myself or to others, and not to think more of myself than I ought to think. There is a happy medium, and I am working on it.

I have ceased throwing up my hands in impatience when the results of my work are not the same as they once were, for I was assured that my talents were being upgraded and that I would be working smartly and simply. I have just completed Luna Number Three, and If truth be told—and it is—I have never been happier with my work.

The Lying Meditation

Preparation:

- Clean your bathroom well, removing all extraneous objects.

- Choose a mat or a blanket on which to lie while meditating in the tub or spa.

- Weather permitting; open the window a few inches for the circulation of fresh air.

- Prepare the tub by adding two cups of bath salts and filling it with very warm water.

- Submerge your choice of mat or blanket in the water. Hold it down until it clings to the bottom of the tub.

- Prepare a cushion on which to rest your head and shoulders, and place it appropriately on the end of the tub.

- Remove your clothing. Place your clothes outside the room and lock the door.

- Prepare a large towel and a warm robe for use at the conclusion of the meditation.

- Climb into the tub and settle your body on the mat and the cushion.

- Lie down on your right side with your right palm under the right side of your face.

- Position your left arm along the left side of your body.

- Drape your left leg gently over your right one. If you are not comfortable, make it so.

- Imagine a spark of light far off in the distance. Focus on that light until your mind is calm and only sees the pinpoint of light. You are ready to begin.

Begin the meditation

- Pray that all that is said and done be to the honor and glory of your Source and for your instruction.

- Return to the spark of light on which you are meditating. Slowly draw it closer to you until it fills your vision with its radiance. Remember, you are not in a hurry. Enjoy the radiance of that light for as long as you wish.

- When that part of the meditation is completed, speak into the light and ask what lesson your subconscious has for you.

- Trust that what comes to mind is a positive lesson from your subconscious.

- Explore that positive lesson, taking time to ask for clarification or further knowledge to implement a plan.

- When you feel that you have exhausted the subject of this lesson, bask in the brilliance of it. It is your authentic self teaching you a subject that your conscious mind may use for your edification. Spend time in this place, and explore it fully.

- When you are ready, refocus on the light as it diminishes in size and slowly disappears.

- You will instinctively know when it is time to open your eyes.

- Only when your mind totally clears and you are sure your conscious mind has taken over completely, may you cautiously leave the bath tub.

- Dry off and don your robe.

Afterthought

This meditation was written for you for the development of trust in what you hear from your subconscious. If you hear a positive lesson, give ear to it. At the same time, there is no reason at all to blindly obey it. Yet do not toss out the thought without considering it, researching it, or adapting it to your specific use.

If you feel that the lesson you hear at the beginning of the meditation is negative, please end the meditation right then and there and open your eyes. In the event this happens to you, you may try this exercise another day to receive better results. Do not entertain the negative lesson for a single moment, for it is not from your Source. I have every confidence in your ability, at this point in your study, to discern whether the lesson posed to you in meditation is for your highest good, or is a negative lesson.

In conclusion, be sure that, above all, you remain in a place of peace.

Chapter 10

Where Is the Music?

The baby grand piano took up half my living room. It jutted into the middle of the room and reminded me every day of the promise I had made to myself. I would finish writing "Passion Forward" before the end of the year. I had hit the proverbial wall about two months prior to the promise and had not yet received the music or the words for this cantata piece.

Music was one of my talents that could not be forced, and I was fully aware of that fact. But, I was not hindered in my attempts. The music that came to mind during this dry period was ordinary and mundane, and as piece after piece floated through my brain, they were discarded.

One morning in early October, I arose in a very interesting mood because a sleepless six hours that night before had rattled me. Music played insistently in my mind for most of that time. There was not one lyric, just the constant playing of the notes to the piece over and over again until I prayed out loud for it to stop. And it did.

The fact that it did stop was no surprise to me, for I had used the same technique for years in other circumstances. I calmed myself with it while inside various banging diagnostic machines and while seated in a myriad dentist chairs. Praying out loud was the only method that allowed me to do either one of them.

I got up, weaved sleepily from the bedroom to the kitchen, and turned on the coffee pot. I sat down at the kitchen table, which faced the windows to the back yard, and waited as the liquid dripped hot and strong into the urn.

When the coffee pot came to a wheezing finish, I poured myself an ample mug of the eye-opener and headed out of the kitchen to the living room with it. I absentmindedly put the mug down on a card that I had placed on the top of the piano the day before.

Finally, I sat down on the piano bench and placed my bare right foot on the pedal. I positioned my fingers on the keyboard and was prepared to play the music that had harassed me for so long the preceding night. I wanted to reproduce the notes that most certainly had burned grooves into my brain. Nothing came to mind. I could not recall the piece that had bedeviled me and caused me to react in anger just a few short hours before.

It was the most frightening situation I had ever experienced. Tears formed in the inside corners of my eyes, but I would not allow them to overflow and spill down my cheeks. This was a temporary problem, I was sure of it.

Bravado has always been an asset to me, and it was so then. "Get a grip," I told myself as I tried hard to remember the music.

Frightening explanations for my current state flashed through my mind, dementia being the chief of them, before I had enough of it and ran to the sanctuary that was my bedroom. I closed the door and threw myself across the unmade bed. What must I do? I had never been in such a predicament before. I could go to the emergency room, but how would I describe my problem? I could tell them that I could not play the piano, but that sounded vaguely like a tired, old joke.

I tried to reason with myself at that point. I found that I could add up columns of numbers in my head and was able to remember words and music to pieces that I had previously written. Based on those two things alone, I decided to try playing the fugitive notes from the night before one more time.

It had been almost an hour that I had been sequestered, trying to convince myself that I was not going mad. I got up from the bed, opened the bedroom door, and walked down the hall to the piano in the living room. I noticed the coffee mug, picked it up, and drank a sip of the cold brew, stalling for time. Then I carefully seated myself before the glaringly white keys with the frequent slits of ebony.

As I placed my limp fingers on the ivories in front of me, only words—no music—came to mind. "Did you not ask that the music be stopped?"

"Oh, okay, turn on the music," I said grouchily.

Not a thing happened that was different than earlier that morning.

"*Turn on the music!*" I shouted to the empty room.

There was not a sound to be heard except my own voice that seemed to echo around the room. Then, another prompt came to mind. It was an unusual word for me to say, one I would never have thought in my conscious mind.

"Unstop," I obediently repeated, for I was ready to try anything to restore the music that I had consciously disassociated myself from the night before.

With relief and a great amount of gratitude, I began to play the longed-for piece of music. I had thought that it was lost to me, but it had seemed so important that I continued the effort to restore it to my conscious memory.

My unconscious mind had stored this piece of music for me until it was wanted by the conscious mind. The only problem I found with that action was that I required the right word to access it. That word was given to me, I trusted it, and the unconscious moved the music to my conscious mind for me. It was simplicity itself, for I had not needed to go into deep meditation. I only asked for the help that I was in dire need of.

The music that had been hiding from my conscious mind was a lovely and inspired tune. I titled it "He Was Taken." It touched me every time I played it, even this morning that I write this, when I rehearsed it.

"He was Taken" became an important and favorite part of "Passion Forward," a cantata that I had written, and I treasure it.

Walking and Standing Meditation

Preparation:

- Give thanks for the instruction to be careful of your words.

- Practice your breathing technique.

- Practice patience with yourself in this matter of breathing.

- Choose an area in which to pace back and forth, about twenty-four steps each way.

- Decide where to stop and stand for meditation and where to begin walking again.

- Check your clothing for comfort and loose fit. Make sure your clothes are appropriate for the weather, because being uncomfortable takes your mind away from the focus.

Begin the meditation

- Cast your eyes downward on the path.

- Begin to walk at a slower pace than you normally walk.

- Be aware of your feet and how they meet the ground. Think only of one foot at a time.

- Notice how your foot rolls with each step as you shift your weight from your heel to the ball of your foot and lift it. Be amazed at the miracle of it. This is your focus.

- Feel the inside of your footwear on your foot or, if barefooted, sense the cool ground on the sole of your foot.

- Let each foot relax as you simultaneously bring it up into the air and put the opposite one on the ground.

- As you finish the extent of your path (twenty-four steps), turn and stand for meditation.

- For your standing meditation, fold your hands loosely in front of you and clasp them together.

- Set the motivation of paying attention to your words.

- Do not be in a hurry, for there is no reason to hurry. Only focus on your motivation at this point.

- See you interacting and communicating with another person. For the purpose of this meditation, let us say you are speaking with a friend.

- Notice your thoughts. You are aware of what you are going to say before you say it. Spend time observing as you practice this important lesson.

- Be gentle in what you say. There is no reason to hurt someone with your words.

- You are now training yourself to be mindful of every word that comes out of your mouth.

- Remind yourself that you do not have to say everything that you think.

- Spend time in this place, and know that this is an important instruction.

- When you are ready, begin retracing your walking path back to your beginning point.

- Again, be aware of each foot and how it touches the ground.

- Now, breathe in tempo with your footsteps. Left foot down, inhale. Right foot down, exhale.

- Meditate on those marvelous feet that God has given you. You move and run and jump with them, and, additionally, they hold you in the standing position.

- You are at the beginning point of your walking and standing meditation. In your walking, your focus is the way you walk, and in your standing, you taught yourself the meaning of true and thoughtful communication.

- You will now stand for a benediction. While you hold the lesson of communication in your clasped hands, you shall say: may the meditations of my heart and mind be acceptable, and the words that I speak, loving. Amen.

- When you are ready, open your eyes.

Afterthought

This story has a few twists and turns, as do most of the stories in this book. But, the main point I want you to take from this story is that the mouth can be a dangerous weapon. It can also be a loving, kind, and gentle way to interact with the people around you.

It is up to you to train yourself to think before you speak and to edit what you say. Remember that "dead air" is not your enemy if you instruct yourself to speak only when you have something to say. Do not be intimidated by a lull in the conversation or feel the need to fill it with inappropriate speech.

As illustrated in the story, do not speak when you are angry. You must simply move in your mind, away from the situation.

This meditation is a combination of the walking and the standing positions for meditating. The walking position is to calm your mind and maintain focus. The standing position is for instruction.

Know that with practice, your meditations will become part of who you are, and you will wonder how you managed your life prior to using them. Feel free to create your own meditations. Make them personal to your daily life, and choose those positions that resonate with you. Be calm.

Chapter 11

Itsy, Bitsy Spider

They are amazing and sometimes a bit sad—the studies that science will perform in order to provide benefit to us humans.

I developed a great interest in physical science as an empty nester in the late 1980s. Then as a retiree, at the age of fifty-eight in the late 1990s, I became an ardent fan of all science-related subjects. The following story is based on a study that caught my eye as I paged through one of my favorite science publications.

Now, I do realize that to reduce this complex study to a few lines in a self-help book is grossly unfair, but here goes.

That particular study was one that, if taken seriously, revealed the physiology of stress. It took you into the world of a tiny spider and proved to you that your responses to stress are very close to those of the garden-variety arachnid.

Subject spider—let us call her Natalie—was weaving a lacey, beautifully formed web from the limb on a small dogwood tree to the crossbar of a clothesline post. It was a sunny day and very warm in the garden that morning, so she took her time to spin just enough web silk to take her swinging back to the tree from her current perch on the iron post. She had made the trip, back and forth, many times that morning.

Once back on the dogwood, she decided to fill in her design with a web so graceful and sheer that she might catch a bug in it for her breakfast. She worked on the miniature bug trap for about an hour. It had to be just right.

The trap was very efficient, and after Natalie had eaten her last bug-meal of the day (a juicy gnat), she crawled down from her position to find a suitable place to rest for the night. The methodical technician was observing it all.

While Natalie was resting in the cozy darkness, the scientist came out of his home, walked over to the small dogwood tree, and shined his penlight upward and between the spindly branches. He finally found Natalie's piece of art—her pride and joy, and he carefully took it with him into the house.

The next morning, Natalie climbed the dogwood tree, up the branch and to the exact spot where her web had been so meticulously fastened. She felt she had made a mistake, however, when she failed to find it. She ran excitedly around the smooth bark of the tree on her eight short legs, trying to find the limb that held her prized web. But, she had been correct in the first instance. The web was simply gone. The tiny spider concluded that there must have been a problem with the construction of that web, and that it had accidentally been carried off by the breeze.

Not too daunted by the loss, she decided to build another web. It was sunny in the garden for the second day in a row, but the wind had definitely picked up, making the spinning of her new web more complex. She had decided to build this web between the eave of the back porch and the banister. The scientist was watching her intently.

Finally, after two hours, her creation fully executed, Natalie sat in a remote part of the web to wait for the catch of the day. She lingered there until it was nearly nightfall. But not one bug came by to test her little trap, and that evening, she went to sleep hungry.

Soon after Natalie had settled down for the night, the screen door creaked as the man let himself out into the night to search for Natalie's web. He found it easily, removed it from between the eave and the banister on the back porch, and walked back into his house with it.

Natalie climbed the porch post slowly the next morning, and when she got to the banister, she looked upward to the eave of the porch. She thought it impossible that the web she had constructed the day before had again disappeared. She scurried back down the banister to the ground and decided to eat some ground bugs for breakfast, after which she would find another place to design and build her third web in as many days.

It was close to evening that day when Natalie came up with her new design and a safe position in which to place it. She decided that the web that she had constructed from the limb of the dogwood tree to the top of the clothes post was her favorite one, so she would build another in the exact same place and in the exact same way.

She hurriedly attached the skein of silk to the tree and spun enough extra web silk to achieve her goal of the top of the clothes post. She swung out into a gentle breeze, fell short of the clothes post and drifted to the ground. This had never happened to her before. She was stunned by the shortfall. Natalie picked herself up, made her way back to the tree, and climbed it.

When she came to the secure place where she had started her web, she looked across to the iron post. Natalie sized up the distance to it from the dogwood tree and made an executive decision not to try to swing across that long distance again. It seemed too far for her to do that. Natalie, suddenly afraid that she would fail in the process of attaching the silk to the iron post, even though she had done so many times before, opted for a change in plans.

She next chose to refasten her web on a small limb that was much closer in proximity to the top of the clothes post. She easily swung over to it in order to attach the other end of the silk to the cold iron. That day, she declined to form a beautiful design as she had previously woven, and instead rode the short distance back and forth from the post to the limb on single strands of web in a rather haphazard way. Natalie had not cared that this creation was neither as beautifully crafted nor artfully balanced as the other webs she had constructed; she just wanted to be done with it. Lastly, she had not included a bug trap in her web, excusing herself from this chore because she was not hungry, anyway.

That evening she left the tree early and descended to the ground to rest, for she was very tired. The scientist was perplexed by her actions, but he waited until nightfall to do his deed.

It was misty in the garden the next morning, and from her vantage point at the foot of the dogwood tree, Natalie spied other webs covering bushes and flowers with gossamer silk. They were beautifully glistening in the morning dew. Natalie climbed the tree to look for her web, not expecting it to be there, and it was not. During the night, the web had again been lifted gently from the small branch of the dogwood tree and the top of the clothes post and transported into the house.

All of her lovely, lacey webs were gone. The ones that she labored on and was proud of and the one that was crudely and quickly done had all met the same fate. She huddled in the crotch of her tree for a while before she slowly climbed it.

Natalie, with little strength of purpose left, decided to spin one more glorious web—the kind she was used to constructing, with separate parts in it for waiting and for catching food. She remembered how pleased she had been with them and how proud she was that she had built them. She selected a site she felt was appropriate to her needs and began to work. Or she tried to, at least. It seemed that she had forgotten how to spin the silky skein required for the basic parts of the web. Having no success at it after a few tries, she decided to try to spin the other, sticky type of threads in which to catch her food. And even though she desperately desired to build just a tiny bug trap, after a few false starts, the disheartened Natalie gave up and dropped to the ground.

To the saddened scientist, it had become all too clear that the study of the spider's reaction to the stress of having her hard work destroyed time after time resulted in the spider's expectation of having it destroyed. The lack of a positive expectation led to complacency, and complacency to depression and brain fog. Ultimately, Natalie was unable to function in the job that she was very adept in doing, and she gave up.

If you can relate at all to some of the preceding parable, you are not alone. Most of us have been to that place of overwhelming anxiety. But, not one of us needs to dwell in that spot for long. I will show you how to move from that situation to a happier and more peaceful one, as you practice the next meditation.

The Sitting Meditation

Preparation:

- Remember to keep your eye on the prize, no matter what others may do to prevent you from doing so.

- This sitting meditation may be practiced out of doors on a sunny day.

- If the day is chilly, wear appropriate clothing, but keep with loose and comfortably fitting clothing.

- Choose a cushion or a blanket on which to sit comfortably. Try it where you plan to meditate to make sure that it is comfortable.

- Place a wind chime close by so that you may enjoy the music of it.

- Stand beside the cushion, shake out your arms and legs, and drop forward from the waist. Let your arms hang from your shoulders for a few minutes. Relax into that position.

- Your focus today is, through half-closed eyes, concentrating on your palms, which will be placed outstretched on your knees.

- The subject of your meditation is achieving a no-stress zone.

Begin the meditation

- Be seated with your legs crossed in front of you

- Breathe deeply, in and out. Be mindful of your breathing, and with each breath, relax more into the pose.

- Lay your arms out in front of you and rest them on your knees, palms up.

- Study them with half closed eyes. Marvel at them, and think only of the outstretched palms in front of you.

- Your palms are a symbol of those things that you do in this life that are true and good. They remind you of the lessons of this meditation.

- Close your eyes and visualize yourself working on a project that you put all your mind, body, and soul into doing. Stay in that place for a few moments. Observe your joy, the unconscious smile on your lips.

- When you are ready, visualize a wrecking ball. It swings back and forth, and each time it swings, the ball narrowly misses hitting your prized project and destroying it. Keep your focus on that wrecking ball. The arc of it brings it nearer and nearing the perceived target of your project.

- How do you feel at this moment? You probably steeled your body against the perceived strike. This is called *armoring*, and it happens when your perception of the situation means the desolation of your completed and hard-earned piece of work. Focus on your place in this vision only until you recognize that this feeling does not put you in the place you want to be in. You want to change that negative vision to a positive one.

- Look again at the swinging ball. The arc has modified. With every swing of the ball, the arc shortens and shortens, until it could not possibly reach far enough to destroy what you have created.

- Now how do you feel? You have been spared, along with your project. The stiff and steely feeling of the "armor" is gone, and replacing it is a feeling of relief and gratitude.

- As you visualize the ball that narrowly missed your project, place it in the palm of your left hand. It is a reminder of the difference in feeling between your perception and an actual happening.

- The delta between perception and actualization is stress. That space in your mind between your perception of danger and something actually happening is stress-causing.

- Return your focus to your palms and the ball that you have placed in your left one. Remember the lesson of the ball, the stress it contains, and the relief from stress it gave you.

- When you are ready and you have learned the lesson well, you may open your eyes.

- Replace the ball in the vision with a rubber bouncy ball and keep it with you for a while as a reminder of your instruction for a no-stress zone.

Afterthought

The story of Natalie, the spider, was used as a natural illustration and was a very real scientific lesson; however, the outcome is far different from the one that you require.

The meditation above deals with the perception of desolation and not the actuality of it. Perception of desolation happens at a far greater rate than the actuality of it. Be advised, though, that whether perceived or actual, either form of desolation can and will make you mentally or physically unwell. Additionally, desolation may transform you into a person unable to perform the work you have chosen to do unless you have a way to relieve it. Obviously, meditation is a great tool to do that.

In the sitting meditation above, you have again used the power of visualization. The large ball, which you perceived to be the stressor, became the small rubber bouncy ball, which is your reminder. It reminds you that most of your perceptions of stress never attain the point of actuality. And if they do, you may go back to the meditation for wisdom. You will ask for a solution to your situation without delay.

Stress, as a word, means nothing and should never be personally used as, "I am so stressed," or, "I had a stressful day." When you say that you have had a stressful day, the speaking of the word, *stress* carves another notch into your brain and builds more stress. Please try this: "I am ready to relax in my favorite chair for a few minutes." Another way to speak positively would be to say: "I look forward to a long hot bath" or "playing with my baby would make me so happy." Speaking in this manner will divert your mind from the negative place of stress to a more pleasurable place and soon the stress will disappear. Train yourself in this technique; you will be pleased by the results. The meditation above is practiced by many people like you and me every day. Remember that you may practice it any time your life requires it.

Chapter 12

Inside the Honey Walls

I was sitting quietly, agitated. The feeling in my gut was excruciatingly tight, as if it were reined in by some unseen tether. That tether was attached to an incident so hurtful that I felt that I would not survive it with mind and body intact.

I had been emotionally beaten in that same place many times in my life, and I would have thought my solar plexus numb by now; so why the drama?

I tried to raise my heavy-feeling body from the chair I was using, but I collapsed back into it hard. I would not be getting up anytime soon. I could not run from the pain, because it was necessary that I deal with my feelings then and there.

To begin this story, I must tell you that the one person in my life whom I believed to be my closest ally and confidant had been cruelly gossiping about me. It was not the usual teasing banter that we all engaged in, but he spoke confidential thoughts and feelings which I had entrusted to him.

This man had proceeded to embellish and color most of what I had told him. He had done so to the extreme, and what he related was very far removed from the truth. I found it surprising that anyone who knew me believed his tales. Furthermore, I was astonished that he could bear to tell them.

I knew these facts because an acquaintance of mine had phoned me with the information that I outlined above. She was only telling these things to me as a friend, mind you.

I confronted my supposed confidant with these stories, sure in my heart that he had not communicated these lies to any and all who would listen. But, I was wrong. He owned up to the complete account given to me by my friend from the phone call. It was just a joke, he said laughingly. It was only to show me how many real friends I had. And it seemed that his stories about me were certainly believed. There were no real friends out there, he had chuckled.

Reliving his horrid explanation in my mind only served to cinch the belly strap and tighten the tether, and I knew that I did not want to repeat it. I just wanted the whole situation to be gone.

I decided not to defend myself. If my friends and neighbors believed the liar's ranting, then I must find new friends. The fact that I had always tried to put forth my true self to my friends and neighbors did not seem to help me. When the lies were told, they were believed.

Instead of defensive action, which would have caused more emotional turmoil, I decided to use prayer and meditation in order to help myself. Looking back on this time in my life, I was startled to find that the first thing I thought of to help myself was not prayer and meditation—it was to display my emotions. I leaned back against the winged back of my chair and closed my eyes. I prayed for myself, I prayed for my former friend, and I prayed for those who believed the lies. As the pain lessened, I gave the whole perceived problem over to God and went into deep meditation.

Once in my meditation, I found warmth and light. I was comforted by the soft, golden amber that surrounded me. I was enveloped in a feeling of blessed safety. No one could hurt me there. No one could reach out an icy finger and stab me in the heart. I was inside the honey walls.

Being inside the honey walls precluded the normal comings and goings of us mortals. To reach me from without, one would have to first touch the amber syrup, feel it melt down the front of his body, then smell the sweet bee-smell that permeated the honey wall. He must taste the otherworldly goodness of the honeyed liquid and, in doing so; experience such joy at what he sensed that his will to do harm to another would be overpowered.

The honey walls work also from within, or they would not function in that same, inexplicable capacity. If I were inside the honey walls and for any reason would want to harm someone, I would be obliged to use my senses in such a way as to know the honey-colored joy, smell the breathtaking bee aroma, and feel the tranquilizing sensation of the amber syrup that would flow the length of my body. I would arrive on the outside of the honey walls with a feeling of gratefulness for the experience of it all. I would no longer be able to allow negative thoughts, feelings, or any awareness other than that of security and love. I would know that need to love and cherish those around me and be unable to move against any human being.

Inside the honey walls is an exquisite space of peace and rest. You have my permission to go there and know it firsthand, if you wish.

The Lying Meditation

Preparation:

- Prepare a small room. Clean it and air it out.

- Make sure that there are minimal distractions, such as extra furniture, in the room.

- Choose loose-fitting and comfortable clothing.

- Remove any makeup or perfume. They can be obtrusive to the meditation.

- Choose a comfortable mat on which to lie. Place a soft blanket on it to cover yourself.

- When you are ready, light a large beeswax candle.

- You will focus on breathing the smell of the beeswax candle.

- The subject of this meditation is loving security.

Begin the meditation

- Lie calmly and quietly on your right side. Draw your blanket up to your shoulder.

- Place your right hand under your right cheek, palm toward your face.

- Put your left arm down the left side of your body and drape your left leg gently over your right one.

- Be very comfortable in this pose, and when you are ready, begin your breathing practice.

- Breathe slowly in and out.

- The first three breaths are shallow ones, and you feel the breath in your nostrils.

- The second three breaths you feel in your chest.

- The third set of breaths comes from the tummy, and the breaths are very deep. Breathe in this manner until you attain the quiet mind.

- Enjoy the smell of the honey as the candle burns. Concentrate on the smell of it.

- Meditate on your security—not the lack of it, only on the abundance of it.

- You are in no hurry, for you are able to find joy in this comfortable, secure place. You are inside the honey walls.

- Meditate on the feeling of warmth in this place.

- Meditate on the beautiful amber light radiating through the honeycomb.

- Meditate on the sweetness of this place as you reach out for a taste of the honey.

- Appreciate the security of the honey walls.

- You feel love for others, for yourself, and for God.

- Be positive, because in the end, you are only responsible for yourself. Not for the deeds of others.

- You will remember this place and come back to it when you have need of it.

- The smell of the beeswax candle will remind you to do so. Light it often.

- When you are ready, open your eyes.

Afterthought

The story that initiated this chapter is simple, but it demonstrates some complex ideas for you to think about. You may consider that my friends' perceived treachery and the decision to discard old friends involved in the lies, was harsh. You may believe that in the same situation you would talk to each person, separate he or she from the group and make your decision based on your gut-feeling about each of them. Of course there is a third way to resolve the problem and that is to simply forgive all of them. Only you will be able to figure that out in the best way for you. Your unique way of seeing and knowing is what must come in to play. I am sure that you will come to your own sense of discernment and find the correct answers for your life.

The lying meditation seems to me to be an excellent choice for this topic. It is a very calm and soothing position to use. I have given you many instructions, so you may not fall asleep during the meditation, but it is certainly alright for you to do so. The meditation will be carried on in your subconscious while you sleep. I have confidence that you took the time to focus on the important points of the meditation and that you found in this meditation all that you desired in order to feel loved and secure. Be calm and find your ultimate security in your Source.

Epilogue

Science has determined that you may on average, use only a small percentage of your brain, as you go about your daily routine. You may certainly turn that around by opening your mind to new and different experiences. This is my point in writing about mind tools in a simple but valid manner. These tools are not used as games or as circus acts, they are real techniques to access the subconscious, where the history of your life and my life is played out from birth and beyond.

I have done a lot of my research in the Bible, because I am Christian, but I have also studied other religions and beliefs and look at the mind tools I write about, in the light of the experience of these convictions.

The Joy Reminder, my first book, was written about Automatic writing. I believe that accounts of automatic writing exist in the Bible. My favorite is in St. John 8: 1–11. This story tells of a woman caught in adultery who was brought to Jesus. When the excited men who surrounded this woman, ready to put her to death, had said their piece, it troubled them to find that he had nothing to say to them. Instead, He did something extraordinary; He knelt to write in the sand with his finger. Whatever He wrote however, seemed to have a great influence on the men, and they suddenly fell silent.

In a short while, Jesus stood. Then He asked for someone to come apart from the crowd who had never sinned and throw the first stone at the woman. When not one man came forward, He knelt once more to finish his writing.

Some scholars feel that Jesus was accessing his subconscious and writing intimate sins that these men may have committed. Others feel that the kneeling and writing gave Jesus time to think. In any case, I rather believe that He had access to His subconscious the same way that all of us do, and it certainly worked for him. Each man silently left the group, the elders first, until not one man stood against the woman.

Finally, Jesus looked up. Seeing that every man had left, He asked the woman where her accusers had gone, and she told Him what He had already known.

Jesus had compassion on her and told her to go and sin no more. To me, this story more than illustrates the way we may use automatic writing in order to ease our situations and resolve our differences.

My research for this book, *Inside the Honey Walls*, had me returning, in my mind, to the books about comparative religions that I had liberated from my former husband's library. In the sixties and most of the seventies, I read most of them, and even though they were hard-to-read Theology text books, I learned to decipher most of the material and learned so much from it.

Lately, I have been reading from a book by William James entitled, *The Varieties of Religious Experience,* subtitled, A Study in Human Nature. It is fascinating that a book written more than a hundred years ago is so valid today. The book contains lectures that were given by James to the students attending Edinburgh College at the beginning of the last century. He writes about so many topics that I know that I would have been riveted to the speaker if I had been able to attend his lectures. Some of his topics were medical in nature, always in comparison with the mind. He addressed the futility of defining religion and felt that personal spirituality was the most valid religion. Churches did not like him very much in his time and still do not for that reason. I could go on, but you must get the book for yourself and begin reading in earnest. You will be amazed at his take on the subconscious mind (he firmly believes in it and writes personal anecdotes to prove that he does).

In my searching, I have found that nearly every major religion in the world suggests that meditation should be part of everyday life. I would encourage you to search and to study on your own. There are more modern books on the subject of meditation than *The Varieties if Religious Experience,* and you can get the titles by searching the web using the key word, meditation. There are more than a few books written about the subject.

The Tao, written many centuries ago by Lao Tzu, stresses the use of meditation in order to exercise the mind, and New Thought, an overall name for those people of many beliefs who come together with the feeling that the mind continues to grow, subscribe to the idea that the static dogma of most religious bodies curtails that growth. They believe in spiritual wholeness through means of prayer and meditation.

Hinduism has as its main practices yoga and meditation, and Moslems, not mentioning meditation as one of the five pillars of faith, practice sessions of prayer throughout the day. Judaism does not list meditation as such, but uses the Wailing Wall, where I am certain many Jews meditate. Prayer is also high on their list.

While Christians do not include meditation in their list of practices, if you read the Bible at all, you will find references to meditation from the beginning to the end of it. In the Old Testament, the book of Psalms is replete with the strong suggestion that we meditate day and night. In the case of Psalm1:2, we are to meditate on the law, and in Psalm 145:5, we are to meditate on the wonderful works of God.

In the New Testament, in the book of 1 Timothy, 4:15, Paul wrote to Timothy, whom Paul called his son in the faith, warning him against the false teachings of the law being done by those around him. In other words, he was supposed to compare and meditate on all doctrine, in favor of what the Apostles were taught by Jesus. In the first two works in this series, I have done all of the above to the best of my ability. I wish you would contact me. I am interested in the way this small and simple book may have helped you. My e-mail is: www. cjsartco@aol.com.

I look forward to publishing the last book in this series, *An Eloquent Echo*. It will contain the use of Confirmation. This final mind tool deals with the messages that you hear constantly running through your mind. These messages may be about you, such as, "I am stupid" or "I am intelligent." Although these confirmations, both negative and positive, are stored in your subconscious mind, they affect the way you consciously solve problems and make decisions. In this next book, you will learn how to overlay the negative confirmations with positive ones by utilizing simple techniques in a radically different way, to produce your required result of a more peaceful and loving life. Until then, I send you peace, love, and joy.

—C. J. Hoffman

978-0-595-48311-2
0-595-48311-9

Printed in the United States
204808BV00003B/196-246/P